ideals®

HERSHEY'S®
Cookies, Bars
and Brownies

Ideals Publishing Corp.
Milwaukee, Wisconsin

Contents

ISBN 0-8249-3023-1
The Hershey Logo is a Trademark of Hershey
Foods Corporation, Ideals Publishing Corporation, Licensee.

Published by Ideals Publishing Corporation.
11315 Watertown Plank Road
Milwaukee, WI 53226
Published simultaneously in Canada.

COOKIE BASICS

General Hints

Measuring

☐ Measure ingredients such as baking powder, baking soda and salt in standard measuring spoons. Level with straight-edged spatula or knife. Do not use kitchen flatware as measuring equipment.

☐ Butter or margarine should be softened before use. Measure by using indicators on wrapper. Recipes are designed for stick butter or margarine. Do not use "soft" or "whipped" margarine, unless specified. Do not substitute shortening for butter or margarine, unless specified.

☐ Measure solid shortening in standard nested measuring cups by packing with a spatula to eliminate air pockets. Level with a straight-edged spatula or knife.

☐ Measure flour and other dry ingredients by lightly spooning into nested measuring cups. Level with a straight-edged spatula or knife.

☐ Measure liquids in a regular liquid measuring cup; read amounts at eye level.

☐ Measure brown sugar by packing firmly into a nested measuring cup with back of spoon; sugar should hold its shape when turned out of cup.

Baking

☐ Preheat oven for five minutes before baking.

☐ Ingredients should be at room temperature for the best baking results.

☐ Check expiration dates on baking powder and baking soda. Aged leavening agents will cause baked goods to rise improperly.

☐ Check oven temperature periodically with an accurate oven thermometer.

Cookie Hints

☐ Use shiny metal cookie sheets at least 2 inches narrower and shorter than the oven.

☐ Do not grease cookie sheet unless specified in the recipe.

☐ Grease cookie sheet or pan by rubbing evenly with a piece of waxed paper or plastic wrap dipped into shortening. Do not use butter or margarine.

☐ Do not use excessive flour when rolling out cookies; too much flour makes cookies dry and tough.

☐ Cookies in each batch should be made the same size to assure even baking.

☐ Cookie dough should be placed on a cool cookie sheet to keep dough from spreading before it is baked.

☐ Bake only one sheet at a time, placed in the center of the oven.

☐ Check cookies at minimum baking time given. Underbaking results in a soft, doughy texture; overbaking results in a dry, hard texture.

☐ Unless other instructions are given, immediately remove baked cookies from cookie sheet with a wide spatula.

☐ Cool cookies completely in a single layer on a wire rack before storing in an airtight container.

Baking Terms

Beat	To combine and make smooth by rapid, vigorous motion using an electric mixer, rotary beater, wire whisk or spoon.
Blend	To mix thoroughly two or more ingredients.
Combine	To stir together two or more ingredients (usually dry) in a bowl.
Cream	To make smooth, light and fluffy by beating with a spoon or electric mixer.
Gradually add	Adding liquid or dry ingredients in small amounts for ease in blending and to prevent lumping.

Cookie Classification

Drop Cookie	Soft dough is dropped by teaspoonfuls onto a cookie sheet.
Bar Cookie	Rich dough is spread in a pan, baked, cooled and cut into bars.
Molded Cookie	Dough is rolled between palms of hands into desired shapes before baking.
Press Cookie	Dough is pushed through a cookie press onto cookie sheet to obtain desired shape.
Rolled Cookie	Soft dough is chilled thoroughly, rolled with a rolling pin on a floured surface and cut out with cookie cutters.
No-Bake Cookie	A molded cookie which has cookie or cracker crumbs or cereal as its basic ingredient and requires no baking.
Refrigerator Cookie	Rich, soft dough is shaped into rolls and chilled thoroughly before cutting into slices for baking.

Cookie Troubleshooting Checklist

Problem	Possible Cause
Cookies do not spread	● dough overmixed ● oven temperature too high
Cookies have too much spread	● oven temperature too low ● cookie sheets greased too heavily
Cookies stick to baking sheet	● sheets not cleaned between uses ● sheets not greased ● cookies underbaked ● cookies left too long on sheets before removal

DROP COOKIES

Chewy Cocoa Drops

Yield: about 4 dozen.

½ cup butter *or* margarine, softened
1¼ cups packed light brown sugar
1 teaspoon vanilla
2 eggs
1½ cups unsifted all-purpose flour
¼ cup HERSHEY'S Cocoa

½ teaspoon baking soda
¼ teaspoon salt
1 cup raisins
½ cup chopped dates
½ cup chopped walnuts
Colored sprinkles, optional

Cream butter *or* margarine, brown sugar and vanilla in large mixer bowl until light and fluffy. Add eggs; beat well. In a separate bowl, combine flour, cocoa, baking soda and salt; blend into creamed mixture. Stir in raisins, dates and nuts. Chill 30 minutes. Drop by teaspoonfuls onto a lightly greased cookie sheet. Bake at 350° for 8 to 10 minutes or until set. Remove from cookie sheet; cool on wire rack.   Decorate with colored sprinkles, if desired.

Chocolate Nut Mounds

Yield: about 4 dozen.

1 block (1 ounce) HERSHEY'S
   Unsweetened Baking Chocolate
⅔ cup sweetened condensed milk

2 cups chopped walnuts
¼ teaspoon vanilla

Melt chocolate in the top of a double boiler over hot (not boiling) water. Stir in sweetened condensed milk. Add nuts and vanilla; blend thoroughly. Drop by teaspoonfuls onto a lightly greased cookie sheet. Bake at 350° for 8 to 10 minutes or until set. Remove from cookie sheet; cool on wire rack.

Peanut Butter Chip Macaroons

Yield: about 3 dozen.

3 egg whites
Dash salt
½ teaspoon vanilla
1 cup sugar

1 cup REESE'S Peanut Butter Chips
¾ cup flaked coconut
Red sugar crystals, optional

Beat egg whites with salt and vanilla in small mixer bowl until soft peaks form. Gradually add sugar, beating until stiff peaks form. Gently fold in peanut butter chips and coconut. Drop by teaspoonfuls onto a lightly greased cookie sheet. Sprinkle with red sugar crystals, if desired. Bake at 325° for 20 minutes. Carefully remove from cookie sheet; cool on wire rack.

Clockwise from top: Crunchy Jumbles, 15;
MINI CHIP Sugar Cookies, 16; Chocolate Chip
Coconut Cookies, 17

DROP COOKIES

Peanut Butter Chip-Orange Drop Cookies

Yield: about 3 dozen.

¾ cup shortening
¼ cup butter *or* margarine, softened
1½ cups packed light brown sugar
2 eggs
4 teaspoons grated orange peel
¼ cup orange juice
1 teaspoon vanilla
3½ cups unsifted all-purpose flour
2 teaspoons baking powder
1 teaspoon baking soda

¼ teaspoon salt
1 cup sour milk*
2 cups (12-ounce package) REESE'S Peanut Butter Chips
¾ cup raisins
1 container (16.5 ounces) ready-to-spread creamy vanilla frosting
½ teaspoon grated orange peel
Red and yellow food color

Cream shortening, butter *or* margarine and brown sugar in large mixer bowl until light and fluffy. Add eggs, orange peel, orange juice and vanilla; beat well. In a separate bowl, combine flour, baking powder, baking soda and salt; add alternately with sour milk to creamed mixture; beat well. Stir in peanut butter chips and raisins. Drop by scant one-fourth cupfuls onto a lightly greased cookie sheet. Bake at 350° for 15 to 18 minutes or until lightly browned. Cool slightly on cookie sheet. Remove from cookie sheet; cool completely on wire rack. Combine frosting and orange peel in small bowl; add red and yellow food color for desired orange color. Frost cooled cookies.

To sour milk: Use 1 tablespoon vinegar plus milk to equal 1 cup.

Soft Banana Chip Cookies

Yield: about 7 dozen.

1 cup shortening
1½ cups sugar
2 eggs
1 teaspoon vanilla
2¾ cups unsifted all-purpose flour
1½ teaspoons baking soda
½ teaspoon salt

½ cup buttermilk *or* sour milk*
1 cup mashed, ripe bananas (about 3 medium)
2 cups (11.5-ounce package) HERSHEY'S Milk Chocolate Chips
1 cup chopped nuts, optional

Cream shortening and sugar in large mixer bowl until light and fluffy. Add eggs and vanilla; beat well. In a separate bowl, combine flour, baking soda and salt; add alternately with buttermilk *or* sour milk and mashed bananas to creamed mixture; beat well. Stir in chocolate chips and nuts, if desired. (Dough will be soft.) Drop by teaspoonfuls onto a lightly greased cookie sheet. Bake at 375° for 8 to 10 minutes or until lightly browned. Cool slightly on cookie sheet. Remove from cookie sheet; cool completely on wire rack.

To sour milk: Use 1½ teaspoons vinegar plus milk to equal ½ cup.

Devil's Food Filled Cookies

Yield: about 16 to 18.

½ cup shortening
1 cup sugar
1 egg
1 teaspoon vanilla
1¾ cups unsifted all-purpose flour

½ cup HERSHEY'S Cocoa
1¼ teaspoons baking soda
⅛ teaspoon salt
1 cup buttermilk *or* sour milk*

Cream shortening and sugar in large mixer bowl until light and fluffy. Add egg and vanilla; beat well. In a separate bowl, combine flour, cocoa, baking soda and salt; add alternately with buttermilk *or* sour milk to creamed mixture; beat well. Drop by tablespoonfuls onto a lightly greased cookie sheet. Bake at 375° for 8 to 10 minutes or until cookie springs back when touched lightly in center. Remove from cookie sheet; cool completely on wire rack. Press cookies together in pairs using 1 to 1½ tablespoons Marshmallow Creme Filling.

To sour milk: Use 1 tablespoon vinegar plus milk to equal 1 cup.

Marshmallow Creme Filling

¼ cup butter *or* margarine, softened
¼ cup shortening
1 cup marshmallow creme

1½ teaspoons vanilla
1¼ cups confectioners' sugar

Combine butter *or* margarine and shortening in small mixer bowl; blend well. Gradually add marshmallow creme, blending well. Blend in vanilla and confectioners' sugar until smooth.

Chocolate Peanut Butter Drops

Yield: about 3½ dozen.

⅓ cup butter *or* margarine, softened
¾ cup peanut butter
½ cup sugar
½ cup packed light brown sugar
1 teaspoon vanilla
1 egg
1 cup unsifted all-purpose flour

½ teaspoon salt
½ teaspoon baking powder
¼ teaspoon baking soda
½ cup milk
½ cup chopped, salted peanuts
1 cup (6-ounce package) HERSHEY'S Semi-Sweet Chocolate Chips

Combine butter *or* margarine and peanut butter in large mixer bowl; blend well. Gradually add both sugars, creaming until light and fluffy. Add vanilla and egg; beat well. In a separate bowl, combine flour, salt, baking powder and baking soda; add alternately with milk to creamed mixture; beat well. Stir in peanuts and chocolate chips. Drop by teaspoonfuls onto an ungreased cookie sheet. Bake at 375° for 8 to 10 minutes or until almost set. Cool slightly on cookie sheet. Remove from cookie sheet; cool completely on wire rack.

MINI CHIP Brownie Cookies

Yield: about 16.

2 cups (12-ounce package) HERSHEY'S MINI CHIPS, divided
¼ cup butter *or* margarine, softened
⅔ cup sugar
1 egg
1½ teaspoons vanilla
½ cup unsifted all-purpose flour
¼ teaspoon baking powder
¼ teaspoon salt
½ cup chopped nuts, optional

Melt 1 cup of the MINI CHIPS in a small, heavy saucepan over very low heat, stirring constantly. Cream butter *or* margarine and sugar in small mixer bowl until light and fluffy. Beat in egg and vanilla. Add melted chocolate; blend well. In a separate bowl, combine flour, baking powder and salt. Blend into chocolate mixture. Stir in remaining 1 cup MINI CHIPS and nuts, if desired. Drop by teaspoonfuls onto an ungreased cookie sheet. Bake at 350° for 8 to 10 minutes or until almost set. Cool slightly on cookie sheet. Remove from cookie sheet; cool completely on wire rack.

Pan recipe

Spread batter into a greased 9-inch square pan. Bake at 350° for 30 minutes. Cool; cut into bars.

Chewy Chocolate Cookies

Yield: about 4 dozen.

1¼ cups butter *or* margarine, softened
2 cups sugar
2 eggs
2 teaspoons vanilla
2 cups unsifted all-purpose flour
¾ cup HERSHEY'S Cocoa
1 teaspoon baking soda
½ teaspoon salt
1 cup finely chopped nuts, optional

Cream butter *or* margarine and sugar in large mixer bowl until light and fluffy. Add eggs and vanilla; beat well. In a separate bowl, combine flour, cocoa, baking soda and salt; blend into creamed mixture. Stir in nuts, if desired. Drop by teaspoonfuls onto an ungreased cookie sheet. Bake at 350° for 8 to 9 minutes or until almost set. Cool slightly on cookie sheet. Remove from cookie sheet; cool completely on wire rack. Drizzle with Vanilla Glaze.

Vanilla Glaze

1 cup confectioners' sugar
1½ tablespoons milk
1½ teaspoons butter *or* margarine, softened
¼ teaspoon vanilla

Combine all ingredients in small mixer bowl; beat until smooth.

DROP COOKIES

Peanutty Date Drops

Yield: about 5 dozen.

¾ cup butter *or* margarine, softened
1 cup packed light brown sugar
2 eggs
1 tablespoon milk
1¾ cups unsifted all-purpose flour
½ teaspoon baking soda
¼ teaspoon salt
¼ teaspoon nutmeg
2 cups (8-ounce package) chopped pitted dates
1 cup REESE'S Peanut Butter Chips
1 cup chopped nuts, optional

Cream butter *or* margarine and brown sugar in large mixer bowl until light and fluffy. Add eggs and milk; beat well. In a separate bowl, combine flour, baking soda, salt and nutmeg; blend into creamed mixture. Stir in dates, peanut butter chips and nuts, if desired. Drop by teaspoonfuls onto a lightly greased cookie sheet. Bake at 350° for 12 to 14 minutes or until lightly browned. Cool on wire rack.

MINI CHIP Sour Cream Cookies

Yield: about 3 dozen.

⅔ cup shortening
1⅓ cups sugar
2 eggs
1 cup sour cream
1 teaspoon vanilla
3 cups unsifted all-purpose flour
2 teaspoons baking powder
1 teaspoon baking soda
1 teaspoon salt
2 cups (12-ounce package) HERSHEY'S Semi-Sweet Chocolate MINI CHIPS

Cream shortening and sugar in large mixer bowl until light and fluffy. Blend in eggs, sour cream and vanilla. In a separate bowl, combine flour, baking powder, baking soda and salt; blend into creamed mixture. Stir in MINI CHIPS. Drop by teaspoonfuls onto a lightly greased cookie sheet. Bake at 350° for 10 to 12 minutes or until *very* lightly browned. Cool slightly on cookie sheet. Remove from cookie sheet; cool completely on wire rack.

Cocoa Raisin Cookies

Yield: about 9 dozen.

1 cup shortening
2 cups packed light brown sugar
2 eggs
2 teaspoons baking soda
1 cup milk
3 cups unsifted all-purpose flour
½ cup HERSHEY'S Cocoa
1 cup raisins
1 cup chopped nuts

Cream shortening and brown sugar in large mixer bowl until light and fluffy. Add eggs; beat well. Dissolve baking soda in milk; add to creamed mixture; beat well. Blend in flour and cocoa. Stir in raisins and nuts. Drop by teaspoonfuls onto a well-greased cookie sheet. Bake at 375° for 8 to 10 minutes or until almost set. Cool slightly on cookie sheet. Remove from cookie sheet; cool completely on wire rack. Frost, if desired.

Peanut Butter Chip Apple Drops

Yield: about 4 dozen.

½ cup butter *or* margarine, softened
1¼ cups packed light brown sugar
1 egg
¼ cup apple juice *or* water
2 cups unsifted all-purpose flour
1 teaspoon baking soda
¼ teaspoon salt
1 cup REESE'S Peanut Butter Chips
1 cup finely chopped, unpared apple
1 cup raisins
½ cup chopped nuts, optional

Cream butter *or* margarine and brown sugar in large mixer bowl until light and fluffy. Add egg and apple juice *or* water; beat well. In a separate bowl, combine flour, baking soda and salt; blend into creamed mixture. Stir in peanut butter chips, apple, raisins and nuts, if desired. Drop by teaspoonfuls onto a lightly greased cookie sheet. Bake at 375° for 8 to 10 minutes or until lightly browned. Cool slightly on cookie sheet. Remove from cookie sheet; cool completely on wire rack.

Chocolate Chip Honey Drops

Yield: about 3 dozen.

⅓ cup butter *or* margarine, softened
½ cup honey
1 teaspoon vanilla
1 egg
1½ cups unsifted all-purpose flour
1 teaspoon baking soda
Dash salt
1 cup (6-ounce package) HERSHEY'S Semi-Sweet Chocolate Chips

Cream butter *or* margarine, honey and vanilla in large mixer bowl until light and fluffy. Add egg; beat well. In a separate bowl, combine flour, baking soda and salt; blend into creamed mixture. Stir in chocolate chips. Drop by teaspoonfuls onto a lightly greased cookie sheet. Let stand 30 minutes. Bake at 350° for 8 to 10 minutes or until lightly browned. Remove from cookie sheet; cool on wire rack.

Peanut Butter Chip Pineapple Drops

Yield: About 3½ dozen.

¼ cup butter *or* margarine, softened
¼ cup shortening
1 cup packed light brown sugar
1 teaspoon vanilla
1 egg
2 cups unsifted all-purpose flour
1 teaspoon baking powder
½ teaspoon baking soda
½ teaspoon salt
¾ cup (8-ounce can) crushed pineapple, well drained
1 cup REESE'S Peanut Butter Chips
½ cup chopped nuts, optional
Maraschino cherry halves, optional

Cream butter *or* margarine, shortening, brown sugar and vanilla in large mixer bowl until light and fluffy. Add egg; beat well. In a separate bowl, combine flour, baking powder, baking soda and salt; blend into creamed mixture. Stir in pineapple, peanut butter chips and nuts, if desired. Drop by teaspoonfuls onto an ungreased cookie sheet. Garnish with cherry halves, if desired. Bake at 375° for 10 to 12 minutes or until lightly browned. Remove from cookie sheet; cool on wire rack.

Chocolate Cake Drop Cookies

Yield: about 5 dozen.

- ½ cup shortening
- 1 cup packed light brown sugar
- 1 egg
- 1 teaspoon vanilla
- 1½ cups unsifted all-purpose flour
- ½ cup HERSHEY'S Cocoa

- 1 teaspoon baking powder
- ½ teaspoon baking soda
- ¼ teaspoon salt
- ½ cup milk
- Confectioners' sugar, optional
- Vanilla Frosting (page 31), optional

Cream shortening, brown sugar, egg and vanilla in large mixer bowl until light and fluffy. In separate bowl, combine flour, cocoa, baking powder, baking soda and salt; add alternately with milk to creamed mixture; beat well. Drop by teaspoonfuls onto a lightly greased cookie sheet. Bake at 350° for 8 to 10 minutes or until almost set. Cool slightly on cookie sheet. Remove from cookie sheet; cool completely on wire rack. Sprinkle with confectioners' sugar or frost with Vanilla Frosting, if desired.

Crunchy Jumbles

Yield: about 3 dozen.

- ½ cup butter *or* margarine, softened
- 1 cup sugar
- 1 egg
- 1 teaspoon vanilla
- 1¼ cups unsifted all-purpose flour
- ½ teaspoon baking soda

- ¼ teaspoon salt
- 2 cups crisp rice cereal
- 1 cup (6 ounces) HERSHEY'S Semi-Sweet Chocolate Chips
- 1 cup raisins, optional

Cream butter *or* margarine and sugar in large mixer bowl until light and fluffy. Add egg and vanilla; beat well. In a separate bowl, combine flour, baking soda and salt; blend into creamed mixture. Stir in crisp rice cereal, chocolate chips and raisins, if desired. Drop by teaspoonfuls onto a lightly greased cookie sheet. Bake at 350° for 12 to 15 minutes or until lightly browned. Cool on wire rack.

Chocolate Nuttys

Yield: about 4½ dozen.

- 3 blocks (3 ounces) HERSHEY'S Unsweetened Baking Chocolate
- ½ cup butter *or* margarine, softened
- 1 cup sugar
- 2 eggs
- 1½ teaspoons vanilla

- 1 cup unsifted all-purpose flour
- ¾ teaspoon salt
- ½ teaspoon baking powder
- 1½ cups chopped walnuts
- Walnut halves

Melt chocolate in the top of a double boiler over hot (not boiling) water. Cream butter *or* margarine and sugar in large mixer bowl until light and fluffy. Add eggs, vanilla and melted chocolate; beat well. In a separate bowl, combine flour, salt and baking powder; blend into creamed mixture. Stir in chopped nuts. Drop by teaspoonfuls onto a lightly greased cookie sheet. Garnish each with a walnut half. Bake at 350° for 8 to 10 minutes or until set. Remove from cookie sheet; cool on wire rack.

DROP COOKIES

MINI CHIP Sugar Cookies

Yield: about 3 dozen.

⅓ cup butter *or* margarine, softened
½ cup packed light brown sugar
¾ cup sugar
1 egg
1 teaspoon vanilla
2 cups unsifted all-purpose flour

1 teaspoon baking soda
½ teaspoon baking powder
½ teaspoon salt
½ cup buttermilk or sour milk*
1½ cups HERSHEY'S MINI CHIPS

Cream butter *or* margarine, brown sugar and sugar in large mixer bowl until light and fluffy. Add egg and vanilla; beat well. In a separate bowl, combine flour, baking soda, baking powder and salt; add alternately with buttermilk or sour milk to creamed mixture; beat well. Stir in MINI CHIPS. Drop by teaspoonfuls onto a greased cookie sheet. Bake at 350° for 10 to 12 minutes or until lightly browned. Cool on wire rack.

To sour milk: Use 1½ teaspoons vinegar plus milk to equal ½ cup.

Brownie Mounds

Yield: about 4 dozen.

6 blocks (6 ounces) HERSHEY'S
    Unsweetened Baking Chocolate
⅔ cup butter *or* margarine, softened
1½ cups sugar
2 eggs
⅔ cup light corn syrup

2 teaspoons vanilla
3 cups unsifted all-purpose flour
1 teaspoon baking powder
½ teaspoon salt
1½ cups chopped nuts

Melt chocolate in the top of a double boiler over hot (not boiling) water. Cream butter *or* margarine and sugar in large mixer bowl until light and fluffy. Add eggs, corn syrup, vanilla and melted chocolate; beat well. In a separate bowl, combine flour, baking powder and salt; blend into creamed mixture. Stir in nuts. Drop by tablespoonfuls onto a lightly greased cookie sheet. Bake at 350° for 10 to 12 minutes or until almost set. Cool slightly on cookie sheet. Cool completely on wire rack.

Chocolate Cherry Drops

Yield: about 8 dozen.

1¼ cups butter *or* margarine, softened
2 cups sugar
2 eggs
2 teaspoons vanilla
2½ cups unsifted all-purpose flour
¾ cup HERSHEY'S Cocoa
1 teaspoon baking soda

1 teaspoon salt
2 cups chopped, well-drained
    maraschino cherries
1 cup chopped nuts
    Maraschino cherries or walnut
    halves, optional

Cream butter *or* margarine and sugar in large mixer bowl until light and fluffy. Add eggs and vanilla; beat well. In a separate bowl, combine flour, cocoa, baking soda and salt; blend into creamed mixture. Stir in cherries and nuts. Drop by teaspoonfuls onto an ungreased cookie sheet. Garnish with cherries or walnut halves, if desired. Bake at 350° for 10 to 12 minutes or until set. Cool on wire rack.

Chocolate Chip Coconut Cookies

Yield: about 3 dozen.

⅔ cup butter *or* margarine, softened
1 cup sugar
2 eggs
1 teaspoon vanilla
2 cups unsifted all-purpose flour
1 teaspoon baking powder
½ teaspoon baking soda
1 teaspoon salt
½ cup sour cream
2 cups flaked coconut
1 cup (6-ounce package) HERSHEY'S Semi-Sweet Chocolate Chips
Sugar
Chopped walnuts

Cream butter *or* margarine and 1 cup sugar in large mixer bowl. Add eggs and vanilla; beat until light and fluffy. In a separate bowl, combine flour, baking powder, baking soda and salt. Add alternately with sour cream to creamed mixture; beat well. Stir in coconut and chocolate chips. Drop by tablespoonfuls onto a lightly greased cookie sheet. Sprinkle with sugar and chopped walnuts. Bake at 350° for 15 to 18 minutes. Remove from cookie sheet; cool on wire rack.

Chocolate Walnut Wheels

Yield: about 2 dozen.

⅓ cup butter *or* margarine, softened
1 cup sugar
1 egg
¼ teaspoon vanilla
2 blocks (2 ounces) HERSHEY'S Unsweetened Baking Chocolate
⅔ cup unsifted cake flour
¼ teaspoon salt
1 cup finely chopped walnuts
Walnut halves

Cream butter *or* margarine and sugar in large mixer bowl until light and fluffy. Add egg and vanilla; beat well. Melt baking chocolate in top of double boiler over hot (not boiling) water; blend into creamed mixture. Blend in flour and salt. Stir in nuts. Drop by teaspoonfuls onto a lightly greased cookie sheet. Garnish each with a walnut half. Bake at 350° for 8 to 10 minutes or until almost set. Cool slightly on cookie sheet. Remove from cookie sheet; cool completely on wire rack.

Crunchy Oatmeal Peanut Butter Chip Cookies

Yield: about 5 dozen.

¾ cup butter *or* margarine, softened
1 cup packed light brown sugar
½ cup sugar
1 egg
1 teaspoon vanilla
1 cup unsifted all-purpose flour
½ teaspoon baking soda
½ teaspoon salt
¼ cup milk
2½ cups quick-cooking oats
2 cups (12-ounce package) REESE'S Peanut Butter Chips

Cream butter *or* margarine, brown sugar, sugar, egg and vanilla in large mixer bowl until light and fluffy. In a separate bowl, combine flour, baking soda and salt; add alternately with milk to creamed mixture; beat well. Stir in oats and peanut butter chips. Drop by teaspoonfuls onto a lightly greased cookie sheet. Bake at 375° for 10 to 12 minutes or until lightly browned. Remove from cookie sheet; cool on wire rack.

BAR COOKIES

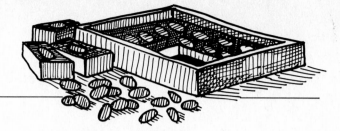

Peanut Butter Chip-Pumpkin Bars

Yield: about 30.

2 eggs
1 cup packed light brown sugar
⅔ cup canned pumpkin
½ cup vegetable oil
1 cup unsifted all-purpose flour

½ teaspoon baking powder
½ teaspoon baking soda
1 teaspoon pumpkin pie spice
1 cup REESE'S Peanut Butter Chips

Beat eggs in large mixer bowl until blended. Add brown sugar, pumpkin and oil; beat well. In a separate bowl, combine flour, baking powder, baking soda and pumpkin pie spice; blend into pumpkin mixture until smooth. Stir in peanut butter chips. Pour batter into a greased and floured 13 × 9-inch pan. Bake at 350° for 25 to 30 minutes or until cookie begins to pull away from edges of pan. Cool completely in pan. Frost with Peanut Butter Brownie Frosting. Cut into bars.

Peanut Butter Brownie Frosting

⅓ cup sugar
¼ cup evaporated milk
2 tablespoons butter

1 cup REESE'S Peanut Butter Chips
1 teaspoon vanilla

Combine sugar, evaporated milk and butter in a small saucepan. Stir over medium heat until mixture comes to a full boil; remove from heat. Quickly stir in peanut butter chips until melted. Add vanilla. Beat until spreading consistency.

Pumpkin-Black Bottom Squares

Yield: about 16.

½ cup butter *or* margarine, softened
⅔ cup sugar
2 eggs
1½ cups unsifted all-purpose flour
1 teaspoon baking powder
½ teaspoon baking soda
¼ teaspoon salt

½ cup sugar
¼ cup HERSHEY'S Cocoa
1 teaspoon vanilla
¾ cup canned pumpkin pie filling
1 teaspoon pumpkin pie spice
½ cup chopped nuts, optional

Cream butter *or* margarine, ⅔ cup sugar and eggs in large mixer bowl until light and fluffy. In a separate bowl, combine flour, baking powder, baking soda and salt; gradually blend into creamed mixture. Divide batter in half. Combine ½ cup sugar and cocoa in large measuring cup. Add to one half of the batter. Stir in vanilla. Spread chocolate batter into a greased 8-inch square pan. Add pumpkin pie filling and spice to the remaining batter; blend well. Carefully spread on top of the chocolate mixture. Sprinkle with nuts, if desired. Bake at 350° for 40 minutes or until brownie begins to pull away from edges of pan. Cool completely in pan. Cut into squares.

Top: Peanutty Cranberry Bars, 22; Bottom: Peanut Butter Chip-Pumpkin Bars, above; Applesauce Bars, 24

BAR COOKIES

Chocolate Coconut Squares

Yield: about 3 dozen.

⅓ cup butter *or* margarine, softened
1½ cups packed light brown sugar
2 eggs
1 teaspoon vanilla
1 cup unsifted all-purpose flour
¼ cup HERSHEY'S Cocoa

1¼ teaspoons baking powder
½ teaspoon salt
½ cup milk
½ cup graham cracker crumbs
¾ cup finely chopped walnuts
½ cup shredded coconut

Cream butter *or* margarine and brown sugar in large mixer bowl until light and fluffy. Add eggs and vanilla; beat well. In a separate bowl, combine flour, cocoa, baking powder and salt; add alternately with milk to creamed mixture; beat well. Blend in graham cracker crumbs. Stir in nuts and coconut. Spread batter into a greased 13 × 9-inch pan. Bake at 375° for 25 minutes. Cool completely in pan. Cut into bars.

MINI CHIP Blondies

Yield: about 3 dozen.

¾ cup butter *or* margarine, softened
1½ cups packed light brown sugar
2 eggs
2 tablespoons milk
1 teaspoon vanilla
2 cups unsifted all-purpose flour

1 teaspoon baking powder
¼ teaspoon baking soda
¼ teaspoon salt
2 cups (12-ounce package) HERSHEY'S MINI CHIPS

Cream butter *or* margarine and brown sugar in large mixer bowl until light and fluffy. Add eggs, milk and vanilla; beat well. In a separate bowl, combine flour, baking powder, baking soda and salt; blend into creamed mixture. Stir in MINI CHIPS. Spread batter into a greased 13 × 9-inch pan. Bake at 350° for 30 to 35 minutes or until lightly browned. Cool completely in pan. Cut into bars.

Chocolate Robins

Yield: about 16.

3 eggs
1 cup sugar
2 blocks (2 ounces) HERSHEY'S Unsweetened Baking Chocolate
½ cup butter *or* margarine
¾ cup unsifted all-purpose flour

½ teaspoon baking powder
½ teaspoon salt
⅛ teaspoon cinnamon
¾ cup chopped nuts
¼ cup raisins

Combine eggs and sugar in large mixer bowl; beat until smooth. Melt baking chocolate and butter *or* margarine in the top of a double boiler over hot (not boiling) water. Blend into egg-sugar mixture. In a separate bowl, combine flour, baking powder, salt and cinnamon; blend into chocolate mixture. Stir in nuts and raisins. Spread batter into a greased 9-inch square pan. Bake at 350° for 20 to 25 minutes or until toothpick inserted in center comes out clean. Cool completely in pan. Cut into bars.

Butter Pecan Turtle Bars

Yield: about 3 dozen.

½ cup butter *or* margarine, softened
1 cup packed light brown sugar
2 cups unsifted all-purpose flour
1 cup pecan halves

⅔ cup butter *or* margarine, softened
½ cup packed light brown sugar
1 cup (5.75-ounce package) HERSHEY'S Milk Chocolate Chips

Beat ½ cup butter *or* margarine, 1 cup brown sugar and flour in large mixer bowl until consistency of fine crumbs. Press crumb mixture firmly into an ungreased 13 × 9-inch pan. Sprinkle pecans over top; set aside. Combine ⅔ cup butter *or* margarine and ½ cup brown sugar in heavy, small saucepan. Cook over medium heat, stirring constantly, until mixture comes to a boil. Boil and stir 1 minute; pour over pecans. Bake at 350° for 18 to 20 minutes or until set. Remove from oven. Sprinkle with chocolate chips. Cool in pan. Cut into bars.

Chocolate Cereal Bars

Yield: about 16.

1½ cups quick-cooking oats
1½ cups crisp rice cereal
1 cup raisins
1 cup miniature marshmallows
½ cup light corn syrup *or* honey
⅓ cup packed light brown sugar

⅛ teaspoon salt
1 cup crunchy peanut butter
¼ cup butter *or* margarine
⅓ cup HERSHEY'S Cocoa
2 teaspoons vanilla

Combine oats, crisp rice cereal, raisins and marshmallows in a large bowl; set aside. Combine light corn syrup *or* honey, brown sugar and salt in a medium saucepan. Cook over medium heat, stirring constantly, until mixture comes to a full boil. Stir in peanut butter and butter *or* margarine; remove from heat. Add cocoa and vanilla; blend well. Pour over cereal mixture in bowl; blend well. Press into a buttered 9-inch square pan. Let stand until cool. Cut into bars.

Yummy Bars

Yield: about 3 dozen.

½ cup butter *or* margarine, softened
½ cup sugar
1½ teaspoons vanilla, divided
1 cup unsifted all-purpose flour
¼ teaspoon baking powder
1 teaspoon salt, divided

1 cup packed light brown sugar
2 eggs
2 cups finely chopped walnuts
1 cup HERSHEY'S Semi-Sweet Chocolate Chips

Cream butter *or* margarine, sugar and ½ teaspoon of the vanilla in small mixer bowl until light and fluffy. In a separate bowl, combine flour, baking powder and ¼ teaspoon of the salt; blend into creamed mixture. Spread into a greased 13 × 9-inch pan. Bake at 350° for 15 minutes. Remove from oven; cool 5 minutes. Combine brown sugar, eggs, remaining 1 teaspoon vanilla and ¾ teaspoon salt; beat until thick and lemon-colored. Stir in nuts and chocolate chips. Spoon over baked layer. Return to oven; bake at 350° for 25 minutes. Cool in pan. Cut into bars.

BAR COOKIES

MINI CHIP-Fruit and Nut Bars

Yield: about 2 dozen.

½ cup butter *or* margarine, softened
1 cup packed light brown sugar
1 egg
1 teaspoon vanilla
1½ cups unsifted all-purpose flour
½ teaspoon baking powder
½ teaspoon salt

¼ teaspoon cinnamon, optional
½ cup golden raisins
½ cup chopped dried apricots
½ cup chopped pitted prunes
½ cup coarsely chopped pecans
1 cup HERSHEY'S MINI CHIPS

Cream butter *or* margarine and brown sugar in large mixer bowl until light and fluffy. Add egg and vanilla; blend well. In a separate bowl, combine flour, baking powder, salt and cinnamon, if desired; blend into creamed mixture. Stir in dried fruits, nuts and MINI CHIPS. Spread into a greased 13 × 9-inch pan. Bake at 375° for 25 to 30 minutes or until lightly browned. Cool completely in pan. Glaze with MINI CHIP Glaze. Cut into bars.

MINI CHIP Glaze

⅓ cup sugar
3 tablespoons water
1 cup HERSHEY'S MINI CHIPS

3 tablespoons marshmallow creme
1 to 2 tablespoons hot water

Combine sugar and the 3 tablespoons water in a small saucepan. Bring to a boil; remove from heat. Immediately add MINI CHIPS; stir until melted. Blend in marshmallow creme. Add hot water, 1 teaspoonful at a time, stirring until glaze is desired consistency.

Peanutty Cranberry Bars

Yield: about 16.

½ cup butter *or* margarine, softened
½ cup sugar
¼ cup packed light brown sugar
1 cup unsifted all-purpose flour
1 cup quick-cooking oats
¼ teaspoon baking soda
¼ teaspoon salt

1 cup REESE'S Peanut Butter Chips
1½ cups fresh *or* frozen whole cranberries
⅔ cup light corn syrup
½ cup water
1 teaspoon vanilla

Cream butter *or* margarine and both sugars in small mixer bowl until light and fluffy. In a separate bowl, combine flour, oats, baking soda and salt; gradually blend into creamed mixture until consistency of coarse crumbs. Stir in peanut butter chips. Reserve 1½ cups mixture for crumb topping. Firmly press remaining mixture evenly into a greased 8-inch square pan. Bake at 350° for 15 minutes. Meanwhile, combine cranberries, corn syrup and water in a medium saucepan. Cook over medium-high heat, stirring occasionally, until mixture comes to a boil. Reduce heat; simmer 15 minutes, stirring occasionally. Remove from heat. Stir in vanilla. Spread evenly over baked cookie layer. Sprinkle reserved 1½ cups crumbs evenly over top. Return to oven and bake at 350° for 15 minutes. Cool completely in pan. Cut into bars.

MINI CHIP-Fruit and Nut Bars, above

BAR COOKIES

Applesauce Bars

Yield: about 3 dozen.

½ cup shortening
1 cup packed light brown sugar
1 egg
1¾ cups unsifted all-purpose flour
½ teaspoon baking soda
½ teaspoon salt
½ teaspoon cinnamon
¼ teaspoon nutmeg
¼ teaspoon ground cloves
¼ cup cold coffee
1 cup thick applesauce, drained
1 cup REESE'S Peanut Butter Chips, chopped
½ cup raisins

Cream shortening, brown sugar and egg in large mixer bowl until light and fluffy. In a separate bowl, combine flour, baking soda, salt, cinnamon, nutmeg and cloves; blend into creamed mixture. Add coffee and applesauce; blend well. Stir in peanut butter chips and raisins. Spread batter into a greased 13 × 9-inch pan. Bake at 400° for 25 to 30 minutes or until toothpick inserted in center comes out clean. Cool slightly in pan. Frost with Lemon Frosting. Cut into bars.

Lemon Frosting

2½ tablespoons butter *or* margarine, softened
1½ cups confectioners' sugar
1½ tablespoons lemon juice
1 teaspoon grated lemon peel

Cream butter *or* margarine and confectioners' sugar in small mixer bowl. Add lemon juice and peel; beat until spreading consistency.

REESE'S PIECES Oatmeal Bars

Yield: about 3 dozen.

⅔ cup shortening
½ cup packed light brown sugar
⅓ cup sugar
1 egg
1 teaspoon vanilla
1 cup unsifted all-purpose flour
½ teaspoon baking soda
½ teaspoon salt
¼ cup milk
1½ cups regular or quick-cooking oats
1½ cups REESE'S PIECES, divided

Cream shortening and both sugars in large mixer bowl until light and fluffy. Add egg and vanilla; beat well. In a separate bowl, combine flour, baking soda and salt; add alternately with milk to creamed mixture; beat well. Stir in oats and 1 cup of the REESE'S PIECES. Spread into a greased 13 × 9-inch pan. Sprinkle with remaining ½ cup REESE'S PIECES. Bake at 350° for 30 to 35 minutes or until almost no imprint remains when lightly touched in center. Cool completely in pan. Cut into bars.

REESE'S PIECES Oatmeal Drops

Follow preceding recipe, except drop batter by teaspoonfuls onto a greased cookie sheet. Place 3 or 4 REESE'S PIECES near center of each cookie. Bake at 375° for 10 to 12 minutes or until lightly browned. Cool on wire rack.

Devil's Food Walnut Bars

Yield: about 16.

½ cup butter *or* margarine, softened
⅓ cup HERSHEY'S Cocoa
¾ cup packed light brown sugar
1 egg
2 tablespoons orange juice
1 tablespoon grated orange peel

1 cup unsifted all-purpose flour
½ teaspoon baking soda
⅛ teaspoon salt
1 cup chopped walnuts
Confectioners' sugar

Cream butter *or* margarine, cocoa and brown sugar in large mixer bowl until light and fluffy. Add egg, orange juice and peel; beat well. In a separate bowl, combine flour, baking soda and salt; blend into creamed mixture. Stir in nuts. Spread batter into a greased and floured 9-inch square pan. Bake at 350° for 25 minutes or until toothpick inserted in center comes out clean. Cool completely in pan. Sprinkle with confectioners' sugar. Cut into bars.

Chocolate Spice Bars

Yield: about 2 dozen.

3 blocks (3 ounces) HERSHEY'S Unsweetened Baking Chocolate
¾ cup butter *or* margarine, softened
1½ cups packed light brown sugar
3 eggs
2 teaspoons vanilla
¾ cup unsifted all-purpose flour

1 teaspoon cinnamon
⅛ teaspoon nutmeg
⅛ teaspoon ground cloves
⅛ teaspoon salt
1 cup chopped nuts
Confectioners' sugar

Melt chocolate in the top of a double boiler over hot (not boiling) water. Cream butter *or* margarine and brown sugar in large mixer bowl until light and fluffy. Add eggs, 1 at a time, beating well after each addition. Add melted chocolate and vanilla; blend well. In a small bowl, combine flour, cinnamon, nutmeg, cloves and salt; blend into creamed mixture. Stir in nuts. Pour into a greased and floured 9-inch square pan. Bake at 375° for 25 to 30 minutes or until toothpick inserted in center comes out clean. Cool completely in pan. Cut into bars. Sprinkle with confectioners' sugar.

Chocolate Date 'n Nut Strips

Yield: about 2 dozen.

2 eggs
½ cup sugar
½ cup unsifted all-purpose flour
1 teaspoon baking powder
6 tablespoons HERSHEY'S Syrup

1 teaspoon vanilla
½ cup chopped pitted dates
½ cup chopped nuts
Confectioners' sugar

Beat eggs in large mixer bowl until thick and lemon-colored. Gradually add sugar; blend well. In a small bowl, combine flour and baking powder; add alternately with chocolate syrup and vanilla to egg-sugar mixture; beat well. Stir in dates and nuts. Spread batter into a greased 9-inch square pan. Bake at 350° for 25 minutes. Cool completely in pan. Sprinkle with confectioners' sugar. Cut into bars.

Chocolate Chip-Graham Bars

Yield: about 2 dozen.

- 1⅔ cups graham cracker crumbs
- ½ cup unsifted all-purpose flour
- ½ teaspoon baking soda
- ½ cup butter *or* margarine, melted
- ½ cup packed light brown sugar
- 2 eggs, slightly beaten

- 1 tablespoon water
- 1 teaspoon vanilla
- 2 cups (12-ounce package) HERSHEY'S Semi-Sweet Chocolate Chips, divided
- 1 cup chopped nuts

Combine graham cracker crumbs, flour and baking soda in a bowl; blend well; set aside. In a separate bowl, combine melted butter *or* margarine and brown sugar. Add eggs, water and vanilla; blend well. Gradually blend in flour mixture. Stir in 1 cup of the chocolate chips and the nuts. Spread batter into a greased 13 × 9-inch pan. Bake at 375° for 16 to 18 minutes or until lightly browned. Immediately sprinkle remaining 1 cup chocolate chips over warm bars. Let stand until chips soften. Spread melted chips evenly over bars. Cool completely in pan. Cut into bars.

Butter Chip Squares

Yield: about 16.

- 1 cup butter *or* margarine, softened
- 1¼ cups sugar
- 1½ teaspoons vanilla
- 1 egg

- 1¾ cups unsifted all-purpose flour
- ½ teaspoon salt
- 1 cup (6-ounce package) HERSHEY'S Semi-Sweet Chocolate Chips

Cream butter *or* margarine, sugar, vanilla and egg in large mixer bowl until light and fluffy. Blend in flour and salt. Stir in chocolate chips. Spread batter into an ungreased 9-inch square pan. Bake at 350° for 25 to 30 minutes or until lightly browned. Cool completely in pan. Cut into bars.

Peanut Butter Syrup Swirls

Yield: about 3 dozen.

- ½ cup butter *or* margarine, softened
- ¼ cup peanut butter
- 1 cup sugar
- 1 cup packed light brown sugar
- 3 eggs
- 1 teaspoon vanilla

- 2 cups unsifted all-purpose flour
- 2 teaspoons baking powder
- ¼ teaspoon salt
- ½ cup (5.5-ounce can) HERSHEY'S Syrup

Blend butter *or* margarine and peanut butter in large mixer bowl. Add both sugars; beat well. Add eggs, 1 at a time, beating well after each addition. Blend in vanilla. In a separate bowl, combine flour, baking powder and salt; blend into peanut butter mixture. Spread half of batter into a greased 13 × 9-inch pan. Spoon chocolate syrup over top. Carefully spread remaining batter over syrup. Use a spatula or knife to swirl batter into syrup for a marbled effect. Bake at 350° for 35 to 40 minutes or until lightly browned. Cool completely in pan. Cut into bars.

Clockwise from top; REESE'S PIECES Oatmeal Bars, 24; Peanut Butter Marbled Bars, 28; Chocolate Chip-Graham Bars, above

BAR COOKIES

Fudge Pecan Bars

Yield: about 16.

½ cup sugar
2 tablespoons butter *or* margarine
2 tablespoons water
1 cup (6-ounce package) HERSHEY'S
    Semi-Sweet Chocolate Chips
2 eggs, slightly beaten

1 teaspoon vanilla
⅔ cup unsifted all-purpose flour
¼ teaspoon baking soda
¼ teaspoon salt
1 cup chopped pecans

Combine sugar, butter *or* margarine and water in a medium saucepan. Cook over medium heat, stirring constantly, until mixture comes to a full boil. Remove from heat. Immediately add chocolate chips; stir until melted. Add eggs and vanilla; blend well. In a small bowl, combine flour, baking soda and salt; blend into chocolate mixture. Stir in nuts. Pour into a greased 9-inch square pan. Bake at 325° for 25 to 30 minutes. Cool completely in pan. Cut into bars.

Chocolate-Almond Honeys

Yield: about 16.

1¾ cups graham cracker crumbs
1⅓ cups (14-ounce can) sweetened
    condensed milk
2 tablespoons honey
2 tablespoons orange *or* apple juice

1 teaspoon grated orange peel
1 cup (6-ounce package) HERSHEY'S
    Semi-Sweet Chocolate Chips
½ cup chopped blanched almonds

Combine graham cracker crumbs, sweetened condensed milk, honey, orange *or* apple juice and orange peel in large mixer bowl; blend well. Stir in chocolate chips and nuts. Spread into a greased 9-inch square pan. Bake at 350° for 30 minutes. Cool 15 minutes. While still warm, cut into bars and remove from pan. Cool bars on wire rack.

Peanut Butter Marbled Bars

Yield: about 4 dozen.

½ cup crunchy peanut butter
⅓ cup butter *or* margarine, softened
¾ cup packed light brown sugar
¾ cup sugar
2 eggs
2 teaspoons vanilla

1 cup unsifted all-purpose flour
1 teaspoon baking powder
¼ teaspoon salt
2 cups (12-ounce package) HERSHEY'S
    Semi-Sweet Chocolate Chips

Cream peanut butter, butter *or* margarine, and both sugars in large mixer bowl until light and fluffy. Add eggs and vanilla; beat well. In a separate bowl combine flour, baking powder and salt; blend into peanut butter mixture. Spread batter into a greased 13 × 9-inch pan. Sprinkle chocolate chips evenly over top. Bake at 350° for 5 minutes. Remove from oven. Use a spatula or knife to swirl chips through batter for a marbled effect. Return to oven and bake at 350° for 25 to 30 minutes or until lightly browned. Cool completely in pan. Cut into bars.

Peanut Butter Chip-Date Bars

Yield: about 3 dozen.

1½ cups chopped pitted dates
¾ cup water
¾ cup butter *or* margarine, softened
1 cup packed light brown sugar
1¾ cups unsifted all-purpose flour

1 cup quick-cooking oats
½ teaspoon baking soda
½ teaspoon salt
2 cups (12-ounce package) REESE'S Peanut Butter Chips

Combine dates and water in a small saucepan. Cook over low heat, stirring constantly, until thickened; set aside to cool. Cream butter *or* margarine and brown sugar in large mixer bowl until light and fluffy. In a separate bowl, combine flour, oats, baking soda and salt; blend into creamed mixture until consistency of coarse crumbs. Press half of crumb mixture into a greased 13 × 9-inch pan. Spread cooled date mixture evenly over top. Sprinkle with remaining crumbs. Bake at 400° for 20 to 25 minutes or until lightly browned. Cool completely in pan. Cut into bars.

Peanut Butter Chip-Granola Bars

Yield: about 4 dozen.

¼ cup butter *or* margarine, softened
¼ cup shortening
1 cup packed light brown sugar
1 egg
1 teaspoon vanilla
1⅓ cups unsifted all-purpose flour
½ teaspoon baking soda
½ teaspoon salt

½ teaspoon cinnamon
¼ cup milk
1⅔ cups granola *or* natural cereal
1 cup raisins
1 cup flaked coconut
2 cups (12-ounce package) REESE'S Peanut Butter Chips

Cream butter *or* margarine, shortening, brown sugar, egg and vanilla in large mixer bowl until light and fluffy. In a separate bowl, combine flour, baking soda, salt and cinnamon; add alternately with milk to creamed mixture; beat well. Stir in cereal, raisins, coconut and peanut butter chips. Spread batter into a foil-lined 15½ × 10½ × 1-inch jelly-roll pan. Bake at 350° for 20 to 25 minutes or until lightly browned. Cool completely in pan. Invert pan and peel off foil. Cut into bars.

Graham Cracker Orange Squares

Yield: about 16.

1 cup graham cracker crumbs
½ teaspoon baking powder
1 egg, slightly beaten
1 teaspoon grated orange peel

1⅓ cups (14-ounce can) sweetened condensed milk
1 cup HERSHEY'S MINI CHIPS
⅓ cup chopped walnuts

Combine graham cracker crumbs and baking powder in a medium mixing bowl. Add egg, orange peel and sweetened condensed milk; blend well. Stir in MINI CHIPS and nuts. Pour batter into a greased 9-inch square pan. Bake at 400° for 25 to 30 minutes or until toothpick inserted in center comes out clean. Cool completely in pan. Cut into bars.

BROWNIES

Hawaiian Chocolate Squares

Yield: about 2 dozen.

3 blocks (3 ounces) HERSHEY'S
   Unsweetened Baking Chocolate
1 cup butter *or* margarine, softened
2 cups sugar
1 teaspoon vanilla
4 eggs
1½ cups unsifted all-purpose flour

½ teaspoon baking powder
½ teaspoon salt
¼ teaspoon cinnamon
1 cup (15½-ounce can) crushed
   pineapple, well drained
½ cup chopped nuts

Melt baking chocolate in the top of a double boiler over hot (not boiling) water. Cream butter *or* margarine, sugar and vanilla in large mixer bowl until light and fluffy. Add eggs; beat well. In a separate bowl, combine flour, baking powder, salt and cinnamon; blend into creamed mixture. Press excess moisture from pineapple. Stir pineapple into 1¾ cups of the batter; set aside. Blend melted baking chocolate into remaining batter. Stir in nuts. Spread chocolate batter into a greased 13 × 9-inch pan. Spread pineapple mixture evenly over top. Bake at 350° for 40 to 45 minutes. Cool completely in pan. Frost with Vanilla Frosting. Cut into squares.

Vanilla Frosting

1 cup confectioners' sugar
1 tablespoon shortening

1 to 2 tablespoons milk
½ teaspoon vanilla

Combine all ingredients in small mixer bowl; beat until spreading consistency.

Chocolate Cream Cheese Brownies

Yield: about 3 dozen.

¾ cup butter *or* margarine, softened
1 package (3 ounces) cream cheese,
   softened
1 cup sugar
1 egg
1 teaspoon vanilla
¼ cup butter *or* margarine

2 cups (12-ounce package) HERSHEY'S
   Semi-Sweet Chocolate Chips *or*
   MINI CHIPS
2¼ cups unsifted all-purpose flour
1 teaspoon baking powder
½ cup chopped walnuts, optional

Blend ¾ cup butter *or* margarine and cream cheese in large mixer bowl. Gradually add sugar; beat until light and fluffy. Add egg and vanilla; beat well. Melt ¼ cup butter *or* margarine and chocolate chips in a small saucepan over low heat, stirring occasionally; gradually add to cream cheese mixture. In a small bowl, combine flour and baking powder; blend into cream cheese-chocolate mixture. Stir in nuts, if desired. Spread batter into a greased 13 × 9-inch pan. Bake at 350° for 30 minutes. Cool completely in pan. Cut into squares.

BROWNIES

Favorite Brownies

Yield: about 16.

½ cup butter
⅓ cup HERSHEY'S Cocoa
2 eggs
1 cup sugar
1 teaspoon vanilla

½ cup unsifted all-purpose flour
½ teaspoon baking powder
¼ teaspoon salt
½ cup chopped nuts, optional

Prepare Cream Cheese Filling; set aside. Melt butter in a small saucepan. Remove from heat. Stir in cocoa. Beat eggs in small mixer bowl until foamy. Gradually add sugar and vanilla; blend well. Stir in flour, baking powder and salt. Add chocolate mixture and nuts. Spread half of chocolate batter into a greased 9-inch square pan. Spread Cream Cheese Filling over chocolate. Drop spoonfuls of remaining chocolate batter onto cream cheese layer. Use a knife or spatula to gently swirl chocolate batter into cream cheese layer for a marbled effect. Bake at 350° for 40 to 50 minutes or until brownie springs back when lightly touched in center. Cool completely in pan. Frost with Brownie Frosting. Cut into squares.

Cream Cheese Filling

1 package (3 ounces) cream cheese,
   softened
2 tablespoons butter *or* margarine,
   softened

¼ cup sugar
1 egg, slightly beaten
1 tablespoon unsifted all-purpose flour
½ teaspoon vanilla

Blend cream cheese and butter *or* margarine in small mixer bowl. Add sugar; beat until fluffy. Add egg, flour and vanilla; blend well.

Brownie Frosting

3 tablespoons butter *or* margarine,
   softened
3 tablespoons HERSHEY'S Cocoa

1 teaspoon vanilla
1 cup confectioners' sugar
1 to 2 tablespoons milk

Blend butter *or* margarine, cocoa and vanilla in small mixer bowl. Add confectioners' sugar and 1 tablespoon of the milk. Gradually beat in remaining 1 tablespoon milk.

Fruit-Nut Brownies

Yield: about 6 dozen.

2 cups (12-ounce package) HERSHEY'S
   Semi-Sweet Chocolate Chips
1 cup butter *or* margarine
2 cups packed light brown sugar
4 eggs
1½ cups unsifted all-purpose flour

1 teaspoon baking powder
½ teaspoon salt
1 teaspoon vanilla
1 cup raisins
1 cup chopped nuts

Melt chocolate chips and butter *or* margarine in a medium saucepan over low heat, stirring to blend. Pour into a large mixer bowl. Add brown sugar, eggs, flour, baking powder, salt and vanilla; blend well. Stir in raisins and nuts. Spread batter into a greased 13 × 9-inch baking pan. Bake at 325° for 45 minutes. Cool completely in pan. Cut into squares.

Sweet Chocolate Brownies

Yield: about 16.

½ cup sugar
¼ cup evaporated milk
¼ cup butter *or* margarine
1 package (8 ounces) HERSHEY'S Semi-Sweet Baking Chocolate, broken into pieces
2 eggs

1 teaspoon vanilla
¾ cup unsifted all-purpose flour
¼ teaspoon baking soda
¼ teaspoon salt
¾ cup chopped nuts, optional
Vanilla Frosting (page 31), optional

Combine sugar, evaporated milk and butter *or* margarine in medium saucepan. Cook over medium heat, stirring occasionally, until mixture reaches a full boil. Remove from heat. Add chocolate; stir until melted. Beat in eggs and vanilla. Add flour, baking soda and salt; beat until smooth. Blend in nuts, if desired. Pour batter into a greased 9-inch square pan. Bake at 325° for 30 to 35 minutes or until brownie begins to pull away from edges of pan. Cool completely in pan. Frost, if desired. Cut into squares.

Chocolate Syrup Brownies

Yield: about 16.

½ cup butter *or* margarine, softened
1 cup sugar
2 eggs
1 teaspoon vanilla
1¼ cups unsifted all-purpose flour

¼ teaspoon baking soda
¾ cup HERSHEY'S Syrup
¾ cup chopped nuts
Vanilla Frosting (page 31) *or* Brownie Frosting (page 32), optional

Cream butter *or* margarine, sugar, eggs and vanilla in large mixer bowl until light and fluffy. In a separate bowl, combine flour and baking soda; add alternately with chocolate syrup to the creamed mixture; beat well. Stir in nuts. Pour into a greased 13 × 9-inch pan. Bake at 350° for 40 to 45 minutes or until brownie begins to pull away from edges of pan. Cool completely in pan. Frost, if desired. Cut into squares.

Double Fudge Saucepan Brownies

Yield: about 16.

½ cup sugar
2 tablespoons butter *or* margarine
2 tablespoons water
2 cups (12-ounce package) HERSHEY'S Semi-Sweet Chocolate Chips *or* MINI CHIPS, divided

2 eggs, slightly beaten
1 teaspoon vanilla
⅔ cup unsifted all-purpose flour
¼ teaspoon baking soda
¼ teaspoon salt
½ cup chopped nuts, optional

Combine sugar, butter *or* margarine and water in a medium saucepan. Cook over medium heat, stirring constantly, until mixture comes to a full boil. Remove from heat. Immediately add 1 cup of the chocolate chips *or* MINI CHIPS; stir until melted. Add eggs and vanilla; stir until blended. In a small bowl, combine flour, baking soda and salt; blend into chocolate mixture. Stir in remaining 1 cup chocolate chips and nuts, if desired. Pour into a greased 9-inch square pan. Bake at 325° for 25 to 30 minutes. Cool completely in pan. Cut into squares.

BROWNIES

MINI CHIP Peanut Butter Brownies

Yield: about 3 dozen.

    3 eggs
1⅓ cups packed light brown sugar
    ⅓ cup butter or margarine, melted
    ½ cup chunky peanut butter
    1 teaspoon vanilla
    1 cup unsifted all-purpose flour

    ¾ teaspoon baking powder
    ¼ teaspoon baking soda
    ½ teaspoon salt
    2 cups (12-ounce package) HERSHEY'S
      MINI CHIPS

Beat eggs in large mixer bowl until thick and lemon-colored. Gradually add brown sugar; beat well. Blend in butter or margarine, peanut butter and vanilla. In a small bowl, combine flour, baking powder, baking soda and salt; gradually add to peanut butter mixture. Stir in MINI CHIPS. Spread batter into a greased 13 × 9-inch pan. Bake at 350° for 25 to 30 minutes or until lightly browned. Cool completely in pan. Cut into squares.

Big Brownies

Yield: about 16.

    ¾ cup butter or margarine, melted
1½ cups sugar
1½ teaspoons vanilla
    3 eggs, slightly beaten

    ¾ cup unsifted all-purpose flour
    ½ cup HERSHEY'S Cocoa
    ½ teaspoon baking powder
    ½ teaspoon salt

Blend melted butter or margarine, sugar and vanilla in a medium mixing bowl. Add eggs; beat well with spoon. In a small bowl, combine flour, cocoa, baking powder and salt; gradually add to egg mixture; beat well. Spread batter into a greased 8-inch square pan. Bake at 350° for 40 to 45 minutes or until brownie begins to pull away from edges of pan. Cool completely in pan. Cut into squares.

ROLO Brownies

Yield: about 16.

    1 cup sugar
    ½ cup vegetable oil
    2 eggs
    1 teaspoon vanilla
    ⅔ cup unsifted all-purpose flour
    ½ cup HERSHEY'S Cocoa

    ½ teaspoon baking powder
    ½ teaspoon salt
  36 ROLO pieces
    1 tablespoon milk
    ½ cup finely chopped nuts

Combine sugar, oil, eggs, vanilla, flour, cocoa, baking powder and salt in large mixer bowl. Beat on low speed until ingredients are moistened. Beat on medium speed until smooth and thoroughly blended, about 2 minutes. Spread batter into a greased 9-inch square pan. Bake at 350° for 25 to 30 minutes or until toothpick inserted in center comes out clean. Melt ROLOS with milk in the top of a double boiler over hot (not boiling) water, stirring constantly. Spread over warm bars. Sprinkle with nuts. Press nuts gently into top of bars. Cool completely in pan. Cut into squares.

Peanut Butter Marble Brownies, 36; MINI CHIP
Peanut Butter Brownies, above

BROWNIES

Peanut Butter Marble Brownies

Yield: about 16.

½ cup butter *or* margarine
⅓ cup HERSHEY'S Cocoa
3 eggs
1¼ cups sugar, divided
1 teaspoon vanilla
½ cup unsifted all-purpose flour

½ teaspoon baking powder
¼ teaspoon salt
1 cup REESE'S Peanut Butter Chips, divided
1 package (3 ounces) cream cheese, softened

Melt butter *or* margarine in a small saucepan. Remove from heat. Stir in cocoa; set aside. Beat 2 of the eggs in small mixer bowl until foamy. Gradually add 1 cup of the sugar and vanilla; blend well. In a separate bowl, combine flour, baking powder and salt; blend into egg-sugar mixture. Stir in chocolate mixture and ½ cup of the peanut butter chips. Reserve ½ cup. Spread remaining mixture into a greased 9-inch square pan. Melt remaining ½ cup peanut butter chips in the top of a double boiler over hot (not boiling) water. In small mixer bowl, combine cream cheese, remaining ¼ cup sugar and melted peanut butter chips; beat until smooth and fluffy. Add remaining egg; blend well. Spread cream cheese mixture over chocolate. Drop reserved ½ cup chocolate-peanut butter mixture by spoonfuls onto cream cheese layer. Use a knife to gently swirl top of batter into cream cheese layer for a marbled effect. Bake at 350° for 40 to 45 minutes or until brownie begins to pull away from edges of pan. Cool completely in pan. Cut into squares.

Best Brownies

Yield: about 16.

½ cup vegetable oil *or* melted butter
1 cup sugar
1 teaspoon vanilla
2 eggs
½ cup unsifted all-purpose flour

⅓ cup HERSHEY'S Cocoa
¼ teaspoon baking powder
¼ teaspoon salt
½ cup chopped nuts, optional

Blend oil *or* melted butter, sugar and vanilla in a large mixing bowl. Add eggs; mix well using a spoon. In a separate bowl, combine flour, cocoa, baking powder and salt; gradually blend into egg mixture. Stir in nuts, if desired. Spread into a greased 9-inch square pan. Bake at 350° for 20 to 25 minutes or until brownie begins to pull away from edges of pan. Cool completely in pan. Frost with Creamy Brownie Frosting. Cut into squares.

Creamy Brownie Frosting

3 tablespoons butter *or* margarine, softened
3 tablespoons HERSHEY'S Cocoa
1 tablespoon light corn syrup *or* honey

½ teaspoon vanilla
1 cup confectioners' sugar
1 to 2 tablespoons milk

Cream butter *or* margarine, cocoa, corn syrup *or* honey and vanilla in small mixer bowl until light and fluffy. Add confectioners' sugar and milk; beat until thick.

Chocolate-Peanut Butter Chip Brownies

Yield: about 2 dozen.

½ cup butter *or* margarine, softened
1 cup sugar
2 eggs
1 teaspoon vanilla
1¼ cups unsifted all-purpose flour

¼ cup HERSHEY'S Cocoa
¼ teaspoon baking soda
¾ cup HERSHEY'S Syrup
1 cup REESE'S Peanut Butter Chips

Cream butter *or* margarine, sugar, eggs and vanilla in large mixer bowl until light and fluffy. In a separate bowl, combine flour, cocoa and baking soda; add alternately with chocolate syrup to creamed mixture; beat well. Stir in peanut butter chips. Spread batter into a greased 13 × 9-inch pan. Bake at 350° for 30 to 35 minutes or until brownie begins to pull away from edges of pan. Cool completely in pan. Frost with Peanut Butter Brownie Frosting. Cut into squares.

Peanut Butter Brownie Frosting

⅓ cup sugar
¼ cup evaporated milk
2 tablespoons butter *or* margarine

1 cup REESE'S Peanut Butter Chips
1 teaspoon vanilla

Combine sugar, evaporated milk and butter *or* margarine in a small saucepan. Cook and stir constantly over medium heat until mixture comes to a full boil. Remove from heat. Immediately add peanut butter chips and vanilla. Beat until spreading consistency.

Chewy Honey Brownies

Yield: about 16.

½ cup butter *or* margarine, softened
½ cup sugar
⅓ cup honey
2 teaspoons vanilla
2 eggs

½ cup unsifted all-purpose flour
⅓ cup HERSHEY'S Cocoa
½ teaspoon salt
⅔ cup raisins *or* chopped nuts

Cream butter *or* margarine and sugar in small mixer bowl until light and fluffy. Add honey and vanilla; blend well. Add eggs, 1 at a time, beating well after each addition. In a small bowl, combine flour, cocoa and salt; gradually add to creamed mixture; beat well. Stir in raisins *or* nuts. Pour batter into a greased 9-inch square pan. Bake at 350° for 25 to 30 minutes or until brownie begins to pull away from edges of pan. Cool completely in pan. Frost with Honey Frosting. Cut into squares.

Honey Frosting

3 tablespoons butter *or* margarine, softened
3 tablespoons HERSHEY'S Cocoa
¾ teaspoon vanilla

1 cup confectioners' sugar
1 tablespoon milk
1 tablespoon honey

Cream butter *or* margarine and cocoa in small mixer bowl until light and fluffy. Add vanilla, confectioners' sugar, milk and honey; beat until spreading consistency.

MOLDED COOKIES

Sunshine MINI CHIP Cookies

Yield: about 7 dozen.

½ cup butter *or* margarine, softened
½ cup shortening
1 cup sugar
¼ cup packed light brown sugar
1 teaspoon vanilla
1 egg
1 tablespoon grated orange peel

2¾ cups unsifted all-purpose flour
1½ teaspoons baking soda
1 teaspoon salt
¼ cup orange juice
1¼ cups HERSHEY'S MINI CHIPS
Sugar

Cream butter *or* margarine, shortening, sugar, brown sugar and vanilla in large mixer bowl until light and fluffy. Add egg and orange peel; beat well. In a separate bowl, combine flour, baking soda and salt; add alternately with orange juice to creamed mixture; beat well. Stir in MINI CHIPS. Cover bowl tightly and chill about 1 hour or until dough is firm enough to handle. Shape into 1-inch balls. Roll balls in sugar to coat completely. Place on an ungreased cookie sheet. Use a fork to flatten. Bake at 350° for 8 to 10 minutes or until lightly browned. Cool slightly on cookie sheet. Remove from cookie sheet; cool completely on wire rack.

Brown-Eyed Susans

Yield: about 3 dozen.

¾ cup butter *or* margarine, softened
½ cup sugar
1 egg
1 teaspoon almond extract

1⅔ cups unsifted all-purpose flour
¼ teaspoon salt
Whole almonds

Cream butter *or* margarine, sugar, egg and almond extract in small mixer bowl until light and fluffy. Gradually add flour and salt; beat well. Cover bowl tightly and chill about 1 hour or until dough is firm enough to handle. Shape into 1-inch balls. Place on an ungreased cookie sheet. Press down center of each with thumb. Bake at 375° for 6 to 8 minutes or until set. Fill center of each cookie with 1 teaspoon Chocolate Filling. Swirl with spatula to smooth filling. Top each with an almond. Remove from cookie sheet; cool on wire rack.

Chocolate Filling

1 cup confectioners' sugar
3 tablespoons HERSHEY'S Cocoa
2 tablespoons butter *or* margarine, softened

1½ tablespoons milk
½ teaspoon vanilla

Combine all ingredients in small mixer bowl; beat until smooth and creamy.

Clockwise from top: Chocolate Cookie Pretzels, 40; Brown-Eyed Susans, above; Sunshine MINI CHIP Cookies, above

MOLDED COOKIES

Chocolate Cookie Pretzels

Yield: about 2 dozen shaped pretzels
or 2½ dozen pretzel sticks.

⅔ cup butter *or* margarine, softened
1 cup sugar
2 teaspoons vanilla
2 eggs
2½ cups unsifted all-purpose flour

½ cup HERSHEY'S Cocoa
½ teaspoon baking soda
¼ teaspoon salt
Confectioners' sugar *or* Cocoa Glaze, optional

Cream butter *or* margarine, sugar and vanilla in large mixer bowl until light and fluffy. Add eggs; beat well. In a separate bowl, combine flour, cocoa, baking soda and salt; gradually add to creamed mixture; blend thoroughly. Divide dough into 24 pieces.

To form twisted pretzels: Shape each piece on a lightly floured surface into a 12-inch rope. Place 2 inches apart on an ungreased cookie sheet. Cross left side of rope over to middle, forming a loop. Fold right side up and over first loop to form pretzel shape.

To form pretzel sticks: Shape dough into 8-inch ropes; split in half lengthwise and twist together or braid. Place on an ungreased cookie sheet. Bake at 350° for 8 to 10 minutes or until set. Cool 1 minute on cookie sheet. Remove to wire rack to cool completely. Sprinkle with confectioners' sugar or frost with Cocoa Glaze, if desired.

Cocoa Glaze

2 tablespoons butter *or* margarine
¼ cup HERSHEY'S Cocoa
2 tablespoons water

1¼ cups confectioners' sugar
½ teaspoon vanilla

Melt butter *or* margarine in a small saucepan over low heat. Add cocoa and water; stir constantly until mixture thickens. *Do not boil.* Remove from heat. Immediately add cocoa mixture to confectioners' sugar and vanilla in small mixer bowl; beat until smooth.

Chocolate Almond Cookies

Yield: about 4 dozen.

1 cup butter *or* margarine, softened
1 cup sugar
1 egg
½ teaspoon vanilla
½ teaspoon almond extract
2 cups unsifted all-purpose flour

½ cup HERSHEY'S Cocoa
¼ teaspoon baking powder
¼ teaspoon baking soda
⅛ teaspoon salt
Sugar
48 whole *or* slivered blanched almonds

Cream butter *or* margarine and sugar in large mixer bowl until light and fluffy. Add egg, vanilla and almond extract; beat well. In a separate bowl, combine flour, cocoa, baking powder, baking soda and salt; blend into creamed mixture. Cover bowl tightly and chill about 1 hour or until dough is firm enough to handle. Shape into 1-inch balls. Roll balls in sugar to coat completely. Place on an ungreased cookie sheet. Lightly press an almond into top of each ball of dough. Bake at 350° for 12 to 15 minutes or until set. Remove from cookie sheet; cool on wire rack.

MOLDED COOKIES

Orange Chippers

Yield: about 10 dozen.

1 cup butter *or* margarine, softened
¾ cup sugar
¾ cup packed light brown sugar
2 teaspoons orange extract
2 eggs
2 cups unsifted all-purpose flour

1 teaspoon baking soda
1 teaspoon salt
2 cups (11.5-ounce package) HERSHEY'S Milk Chocolate Chips
1 cup chopped nuts

Cream butter *or* margarine, both sugars and orange extract in large mixer bowl until light and fluffy. Add eggs; beat well. In a separate bowl, combine flour, baking soda and salt; gradually add to creamed mixture; beat well. Stir in chocolate chips and nuts. Shape into 1-inch balls. Place on an ungreased cookie sheet. Bake at 375° for 10 to 12 minutes or until lightly browned. Remove to wire rack to cool.

Milk Chocolate Chip-Peanut Butter Cookies

Yield: about 8 dozen.

½ cup butter *or* margarine, softened
½ cup shortening
1 cup peanut butter
1 cup packed light brown sugar
1 cup sugar
2 eggs
1 teaspoon vanilla

2½ cups unsifted all-purpose flour
1½ teaspoons baking soda
1 teaspoon baking powder
½ teaspoon salt
2 cups (11.5-ounce package) HERSHEY'S Milk Chocolate Chips

Cream butter *or* margarine, shortening, peanut butter, both sugars, eggs and vanilla in large mixer bowl until light and fluffy. In a separate bowl, combine flour, baking soda, baking powder and salt; gradually add to creamed mixture; beat well. Stir in chocolate chips. Shape into 1-inch balls. Place on an ungreased cookie sheet. Use a fork to flatten. Bake at 375° for 10 to 12 minutes or until almost set. Cool slightly on cookie sheet. Remove from cookie sheet; cool completely on wire rack.

Nutty MINI CHIP Balls

Yield: about 5 dozen.

1 cup butter *or* margarine, softened
½ cup sugar
1 teaspoon vanilla
2 cups unsifted all-purpose flour
¼ teaspoon salt

2 cups (12-ounce package) HERSHEY'S MINI CHIPS
1 egg white
1 tablespoon water
1 cup flaked coconut *or* finely chopped nuts

Cream butter *or* margarine, sugar and vanilla in large mixer bowl until light and fluffy. Blend in flour and salt. Stir in MINI CHIPS. Shape into 1-inch balls. (Chill dough if too soft to handle.) Beat egg white with water until foamy. Dip balls in egg white mixture, then in coconut *or* nuts to coat completely. Place on a greased cookie sheet. Bake at 350° for 16 to 18 minutes or until lightly browned. Remove from cookie sheet; cool on wire rack.

Home Run Smackers

Yield: about 2½ dozen.

1 cup wheat flakes cereal
½ cup butter *or* margarine, softened
½ cup peanut butter
½ cup sugar
¼ cup milk

1 cup unsifted all-purpose flour
½ teaspoon baking soda
¼ teaspoon salt
36 HERSHEY'S KISSES

Crush cereal to measure ½ cup; set aside. Cream butter *or* margarine, peanut butter and sugar in large mixer bowl until light and fluffy. Add milk; beat well. Stir in crushed cereal, flour, baking soda and salt. Shape into 1-inch balls. Place on an ungreased cookie sheet. Use the tip of a teaspoon to make a shallow indentation in top of each ball. Bake at 350° for 10 to 12 minutes or until almost set. Remove from oven; press an unwrapped KISS in the center of each cookie. Cool 2 minutes on cookie sheet. Remove from cookie sheet; cool completely on wire rack.

Peanutty-Apricot Frosties

Yield: about 2 dozen.

½ cup butter *or* margarine, softened
⅓ cup confectioners' sugar
1 tablespoon water
1 teaspoon vanilla
1¼ cups unsifted all-purpose flour

1 cup REESE'S Peanut Butter Chips, chopped*
½ cup finely chopped dried apricots
Confectioners' sugar

Cream butter *or* margarine, confectioners' sugar, water and vanilla in large mixer bowl until light and fluffy. Blend in flour. Stir in chopped peanut butter chips and apricots. Shape into 1-inch balls. Place on an ungreased cookie sheet. Bake at 300° for 18 to 20 minutes or until lightly browned. Remove from cookie sheet. Roll in confectioners' sugar. Cool completely on wire rack.

*Do not chop peanut butter chips in food processor or blender.

Spiked Peanut Butter Chip-Cinnamon Balls

Yield: about 4½ dozen.

1 cup butter *or* margarine, softened
1 cup confectioners' sugar
½ teaspoon vanilla
2 cups unsifted all-purpose flour

2 tablespoons Triple Sec
1 cup REESE'S Peanut Butter Chips, chopped*
Cinnamon

Cream butter *or* margarine, confectioners' sugar and vanilla in large mixer bowl until light and fluffy. Blend in flour and Triple Sec. Stir in chopped peanut butter chips. Shape into 1-inch balls. Place on an ungreased cookie sheet. Sprinkle with cinnamon. Bake at 325° for 18 to 20 minutes or until lightly browned. Remove from cookie sheet; cool on wire rack.

*Do not chop peanut butter chips in food processor or blender.

MOLDED COOKIES

Chocolate Cobblestone Cookies

Yield: about 5 dozen.

½ cup butter *or* margarine, softened
1 package (3 ounces) cream cheese, softened
1 cup sugar
1 egg
1 teaspoon vanilla

2 cups (12-ounce package) HERSHEY'S Semi-Sweet Chocolate Chips
¼ cup butter *or* margarine
2½ cups unsifted all-purpose flour
1 teaspoon baking soda

Blend ½ cup butter *or* margarine and cream cheese in large mixer bowl until smooth. Gradually add sugar; beat until light and fluffy. Beat in egg and vanilla. Melt chocolate chips and ¼ cup butter *or* margarine in the top of a double boiler over hot (not boiling) water. Gradually add to creamed mixture; beat well. In a separate bowl, combine flour and baking soda; gradually add to chocolate mixture; beat well. Cover bowl tightly and chill several hours or overnight. Shape into 1-inch balls. Place on a lightly greased cookie sheet. Use a glass to flatten slightly. Bake at 375° for 8 to 10 minutes or until almost set. Cool slightly on cookie sheet. Remove from cookie sheet; cool completely on wire rack.

Thumbprint KISS Cookies

Yield: about 2½ dozen.

½ cup butter *or* margarine, softened
½ cup sugar
1 egg yolk
2 tablespoons milk
1 teaspoon vanilla
1 cup unsifted all-purpose flour

⅓ cup HERSHEY'S Cocoa
¼ teaspoon salt
½ cup ground nuts
1 tablespoon sugar
36 HERSHEY'S KISSES (6-ounce package), unwrapped

Cream butter *or* margarine, ½ cup sugar, egg yolk, milk and vanilla in large mixer bowl until light and fluffy. In a small bowl, combine flour, cocoa and salt; gradually add to creamed mixture; beat well. Cover bowl tightly and chill about 1 hour or until dough is firm enough to handle. Shape into 1-inch balls. In a small bowl, combine nuts and 1 tablespoon sugar. Roll balls in nut-sugar mixture to coat completely. Place on a greased cookie sheet. Press down center of each with thumb. Bake at 350° for 10 to 12 minutes or until set. Fill center of each cookie with ¼ teaspoon Thumbprint Filling. Immediately press unwrapped KISS into Filling. Remove from cookie sheet; cool on wire rack.

Thumbprint Filling

½ cup confectioners' sugar
1 tablespoon butter *or* margarine, softened

2 teaspoons milk
¼ teaspoon vanilla

Combine all ingredients in small mixer bowl; beat until smooth and creamy.

Cocoa-Glazed Cherry Cookies

Yield: about 3 dozen.

½ cup butter *or* margarine, softened	⅓ cup HERSHEY'S Cocoa
1 cup sugar	¾ teaspoon baking soda
1 egg	¼ teaspoon salt
1 teaspoon vanilla	½ cup chopped, well-drained
1¼ cups unsifted all-purpose flour	maraschino cherries

Cream butter *or* margarine and sugar in large mixer bowl until light and fluffy. Add egg and vanilla; beat well. In a separate bowl, combine flour, cocoa, baking soda and salt; gradually add to creamed mixture; beat well. Stir in cherries. Cover bowl tightly and chill several hours or overnight. Shape into 1-inch balls. Place on an ungreased cookie sheet. Bake at 375° for 8 to 10 minutes or until set. Remove from cookie sheet; cool on wire rack. Frost with Cocoa Cookie Frosting.

Cocoa Cookie Frosting

¼ cup HERSHEY'S Cocoa	2 tablespoons butter *or* margarine
3 tablespoons water	½ teaspoon vanilla
1 tablespoon light corn syrup	1 cup confectioners' sugar

Combine cocoa, water, corn syrup and butter *or* margarine in a small saucepan. Cook over low heat, stirring constantly, until mixture thickens. Remove from heat. Stir in vanilla. Gradually add confectioners' sugar; beat until smooth.

Short KISS Cookies

Yield: about 2 dozen.

1 package (3 ounces) cream cheese, softened	½ cup sugar
¼ cup butter *or* margarine, softened	¼ teaspoon grated lemon peel
¼ cup shortening	1 tablespoon lemon juice
1 cup unsifted all-purpose flour	½ cup finely chopped pecans
1 egg, slightly beaten	24 HERSHEY'S KISSES

Combine cream cheese, butter *or* margarine and shortening in small mixer bowl. Blend in flour. Shape dough into 24 1-inch balls. Place in ungreased 1¾-inch muffin cups. Press balls against the bottom and up the side of muffin cups; set aside. Combine egg, sugar, lemon peel, lemon juice and nuts in a small mixing bowl. Fill pastry-lined muffin cups half full with filling. Bake at 350° for 20 to 25 minutes, or until pastry is golden. Remove from oven. Immediately press an unwrapped KISS into each tart. (After 3 to 5 minutes, chocolate can be spread to cover entire cookie, if desired.) Cool about 30 minutes in pan. Remove from pan; cool completely.

REFRIGERATOR COOKIES

Choco-Cherry Flags

Yield: about 8 dozen.

1 cup (6-ounce package) HERSHEY'S Semi-Sweet Chocolate Chips
1 cup butter *or* margarine, softened
1½ cups sugar
1 egg
1 teaspoon vanilla
2½ cups unsifted all-purpose flour
1½ teaspoons baking powder
½ teaspoon salt
⅓ cup chopped, red candied cherries
½ teaspoon almond extract

Melt chocolate chips in the top of a double boiler over hot (not boiling) water. Cream butter *or* margarine and sugar in large mixer bowl until light and fluffy. Add egg and vanilla; beat well. In a separate bowl, combine flour, baking powder and salt; gradually add to creamed mixture; beat well. Divide dough into thirds. Combine one-third of the dough with candied cherries and almond extract; blend well. Add melted chocolate to remaining two-thirds dough; blend well. Line a 9 × 5-inch loaf pan with waxed paper. Press half of the chocolate dough firmly into prepared pan. Press cherry dough on top of chocolate dough. Press remaining chocolate dough on top. Cover pan tightly; chill several hours or overnight. Carefully remove dough from pan by pulling on edges of waxed paper. Cut dough in half lengthwise. Slice each half into ¼-inch thick slices. Place on an ungreased cookie sheet. Bake at 400° for 8 to 10 minutes or until almost set. Cool slightly on cookie sheet. Remove from cookie sheet; cool completely on wire rack.

Pinwheel Cookies

Yield: about 3 dozen.

½ cup butter *or* margarine, softened
1 package (3 ounces) cream cheese, softened
1 cup sugar
1 egg
1 teaspoon vanilla
2¼ cups unsifted all-purpose flour, divided
½ teaspoon baking powder
½ teaspoon salt
⅛ teaspoon baking soda
½ cup HERSHEY'S Cocoa

Cream butter *or* margarine, cream cheese, sugar, egg and vanilla in large mixer bowl until light and fluffy. In a separate bowl, combine 1½ cups of the flour, baking powder, salt and baking soda; blend into creamed mixture. Divide dough in half. Add cocoa to one half of dough; blend well. Add ¾ cup flour to remaining half of dough; blend well. Roll each half into a 9-inch square. (If dough is too soft, chill about 15 minutes.) Place chocolate dough on top of vanilla. Roll up jelly-roll style. Wrap tightly in waxed paper; chill several hours or overnight. Slice dough ¼ inch thick. Place on an ungreased cookie sheet. Bake at 350° for 12 to 15 minutes or until lightly browned. Remove from cookie sheet; cool on wire rack.

Choco-Cherry Flags, above; Pinwheel Cookies, above

REFRIGERATOR COOKIES

MINI CHIP Slice-And-Bake Cookies

Yield: about 6 dozen.

⅓ cup butter *or* margarine, softened
¾ cup sugar
½ cup packed light brown sugar
1 egg
1 teaspoon vanilla
2½ cups unsifted all-purpose flour

1 teaspoon baking soda
½ teaspoon baking powder
½ teaspoon salt
2 to 3 tablespoons milk
1 cup HERSHEY'S MINI CHIPS

Cream butter *or* margarine and both sugars in large mixer bowl until light and fluffy. Add egg and vanilla; beat well. In a separate bowl, combine flour, baking soda, baking powder and salt; blend into creamed mixture. Blend in milk, 1 tablespoon at a time, until mixture holds together. Stir in MINI CHIPS. Divide dough in half. Shape each half into a 1½-inch thick roll. Wrap in waxed paper; chill several hours or overnight. Slice dough ¼ inch thick. Place on a greased cookie sheet. Bake at 350° for 8 to 10 minutes or until set. Remove from cookie sheet; cool on wire rack.

Chewy Chocolate Wafer Rounds

Yield: about 3½ dozen.

½ cup butter *or* margarine, softened
1 cup sugar
1 egg
1 teaspoon vanilla
1¼ cups unsifted all-purpose flour

⅓ cup HERSHEY'S Cocoa
¾ teaspoon baking soda
¼ teaspoon salt
Chopped nuts *or* flaked coconut, optional

Cream butter *or* margarine and sugar in large mixer bowl until light and fluffy. Add egg and vanilla; beat well. In a separate bowl, combine flour, cocoa, baking soda and salt; gradually add to creamed mixture; beat well. Shape into a 1½-inch wide roll. (Dough will be soft.) Wrap tightly in waxed paper; chill several hours or overnight. Slice dough ¼ inch thick. Place on an ungreased cookie sheet. Sprinkle with chopped nuts *or* flaked coconut, if desired. Bake at 375° for 8 to 10 minutes or until set. Remove from cookie sheet; cool on wire rack.

Cocoa Gingerbread Cookies

Yield: about 4 dozen.

1 cup butter *or* margarine, softened
½ cup sugar
¾ cup molasses
1 egg

1 teaspoon vanilla
3½ cups unsifted all-purpose flour
½ cup HERSHEY'S Cocoa
½ teaspoon baking soda

Cream butter *or* margarine and sugar in large mixer bowl until light and fluffy. Add molasses, egg and vanilla; blend well. In a separate bowl, combine flour, cocoa and baking soda; gradually add to creamed mixture; beat well. Cover bowl tightly; chill about 2 hours or until firm enough to roll. Roll a small amount of dough at a time ¼ inch thick on lightly floured surface; cut into desired shapes. Place on lightly greased cookie sheet. Bake at 350° for 7 to 8 minutes or until set. Remove from cookie sheet; cool on wire rack.

Slice-and-Bake Peanut Butter and MINI CHIP Cookies

Yield: about 8 dozen.

½ cup butter *or* margarine, softened
½ cup shortening
1 cup sugar
¾ cup packed light brown sugar
2 eggs
1 teaspoon vanilla

2½ cups unsifted all-purpose flour
1 teaspoon baking soda
½ teaspoon salt
1 cup REESE'S Peanut Butter Chips
1 cup HERSHEY'S MINI CHIPS

Cream butter *or* margarine, shortening, both sugars, eggs and vanilla in large mixer bowl until light and fluffy. In a separate bowl, combine flour, baking soda and salt; gradually add to creamed mixture; beat well. Stir in peanut butter chips and MINI CHIPS. Chill until dough is firm enough to handle. Divide dough in half. Shape each half into a 2-inch thick roll. Wrap tightly in waxed paper; chill several hours or overnight. Slice dough 1 inch thick. Cut each slice into four quarters. Place on an ungreased cookie sheet. Bake at 375° for 8 to 10 minutes or until lightly browned. Remove from cookie sheet; cool on wire rack.

NOTE: Rolls wrapped tightly in foil can be frozen up to 8 weeks. To bake, thaw rolls just enough to slice easily. Bake as directed above.

Chocolate Sandwich Cookies

Yield: about 3 dozen.

½ cup butter *or* margarine, softened
1 cup sugar
1 egg
1 teaspoon vanilla

1¼ cups unsifted all-purpose flour
½ cup HERSHEY'S Cocoa
¾ teaspoon baking soda
¼ teaspoon salt

Cream butter *or* margarine, sugar, egg and vanilla in large mixer bowl until light and fluffy. In a separate bowl, combine flour, cocoa, baking soda and salt; blend into creamed mixture. Divide dough in half. Shape each half into a 1½-inch thick roll. Wrap in waxed paper; chill several hours or overnight. Slice dough ⅛ inch thick. Place on an ungreased cookie sheet. Draw tines of a fork across each slice to decorate. Bake at 375° for 8 to 10 minutes or until almost set. Cool slightly on cookie sheet. Remove from cookie sheet; cool completely on wire rack. Spread one cookie with Creamy Filling; top with a second cookie.

Creamy Filling

2½ cups confectioners' sugar
¼ cup butter *or* margarine, softened

2 tablespoons milk
1 teaspoon vanilla

Combine all ingredients in small mixer bowl; beat until smooth and creamy.

NO-BAKE COOKIES

Peanut Butter Drops

Yield: about 2½ dozen.

1 cup (6-ounce package) HERSHEY'S Semi-Sweet Chocolate Chips
⅔ cup sweetened condensed milk
½ cup miniature marshmallows
¼ cup peanut butter
1 teaspoon vanilla
½ cup coarsely chopped peanuts

Melt chocolate in the top of a double boiler over hot (not boiling) water. Stir in sweetened condensed milk and marshmallows. Cook, stirring constantly, until marshmallows are melted and mixture is smooth. Remove from heat. Stir in peanut butter, vanilla and chopped peanuts. Spoon mixture into small fluted candy cups.

Chocolate Rum Balls

Yield: about 4 dozen.

1 package (12 ounces) vanilla wafers, crushed (3¼ cups)
¾ cup confectioners' sugar
¼ cup HERSHEY'S Cocoa
1½ cups chopped nuts
3 tablespoons light corn syrup
½ cup rum or ½ cup orange juice plus 1 teaspooon grated orange peel
Confectioners' sugar

Combine crushed vanilla wafers, ¾ cup confectioners' sugar, cocoa and nuts in a large bowl. Blend in corn syrup and rum or orange juice and peel . Shape into 1-inch balls. Roll balls in confectioners' sugar to coat completely. Store in an airtight container for 3 to 4 days to develop flavor. Roll again in confectioners' sugar before serving.

No-Bake Cocoa Crunch Squares

Yield: about 16.

½ cup peanut butter
¼ cup HERSHEY'S Cocoa
½ cup sugar
½ cup light corn syrup or honey
3 cups cereal (2 cups bite-size crisp rice squares or bite size honey graham squares plus 1 cup granola)
¼ cup unsalted peanuts, raisins or chopped pitted dates, optional

Combine peanut butter and cocoa in a small bowl; blend well; set aside. Combine sugar and corn syrup or honey in a medium saucepan. Cook and stir over medium heat until mixture comes to a boil; boil 1 minute. Remove from heat. Add chocolate-peanut butter mixture; stir until well blended. Add cereal and peanuts, raisins or dates, if desired; toss to coat cereal evenly. Spread mixture into a buttered 8-inch square pan. Cool. Cut into squares.

Peanut Butter Drops, above; Chocolate Rum Balls, above

NO-BAKE COOKIES

Chocolate-Orange Nutties

Yield: about 4 dozen.

2 cups (11.5-ounce package) HERSHEY'S Milk Chocolate Chips
3 tablespoons light corn syrup
½ cup orange juice
½ teaspoon grated orange peel
1 package (12 ounces) vanilla wafers, crushed (3¼ cups)
½ cup confectioners' sugar
1 cup finely chopped nuts
Confectioners' sugar

Melt milk chocolate chips in the top of a double boiler over hot (not boiling) water. Remove from heat. Stir in corn syrup, orange juice and peel. In a separate bowl, combine crushed vanilla wafers, confectioners' sugar and nuts. Add to chocolate mixture; mix well. Let stand 30 minutes. Shape into 1-inch balls. Roll balls in confectioners' sugar.

Rich Cocoa Balls

Yield: about 5 dozen.

3½ cups confectioners' sugar
¾ cup HERSHEY'S Cocoa
1⅓ cups (14-ounce can) sweetened condensed milk
1 teaspoon vanilla
2 cups finely chopped walnuts
Confectioners' sugar

Combine confectioners' sugar and cocoa in large mixer bowl. Add sweetened condensed milk and vanilla; blend well. Stir in nuts. Cover bowl tightly; chill about 30 minutes. Shape into 1-inch balls. Roll in confectioners' sugar to coat completely. Place in storage container. Cover tightly; chill at least 2 hours or until firm.

Chocolate-Coconutties

Yield: about 1½ dozen.

1½ cups vanilla wafer cookie crumbs
⅔ cup flaked coconut
⅔ cup confectioners' sugar
½ cup (5.5-ounce can) HERSHEY'S Syrup
1 teaspoon vanilla
Confectioners' sugar

Combine vanilla wafer crumbs, coconut and confectioners' sugar in a medium bowl. Add chocolate syrup and vanilla; mix well. Shape into 1-inch balls. Roll balls in confectioners' sugar to coat completely. Store in an airtight container lined with waxed paper. Roll again in confectioners' sugar before serving.

Peanut Butter Cereal Squares

Yield: about 2 dozen.

- 1 cup light corn syrup
- ⅔ cup packed light brown sugar
- 2 cups (12-ounce package) REESE'S Peanut Butter Chips
- 2 tablespoons vegetable oil
- 2 teaspoons vanilla
- 4 cups crisp rice cereal
- 2 cups corn flakes, lightly crushed

Combine corn syrup and brown sugar in a large saucepan; bring to a full boil over medium heat, stirring constantly. Add peanut butter chips and oil; stir until chips are melted. Remove from heat; stir in vanilla. Add crisp rice cereal and corn flakes; stir to coat thoroughly. Press into a buttered 13 × 9-inch pan. Cool completely; cut into squares.

No-Bake Peanut Butter Chip Cookies

Yield: about 2 dozen.

- 2 cups (12-ounce package) REESE'S Peanut Butter Chips
- 1 tablespoon shortening
- 5 cups corn flakes cereal, coarsely crushed
- 1 cup raisins

Melt peanut butter chips and shortening in the top of a double boiler over hot (not boiling) water, stirring until smooth and creamy. Stir in crushed corn flakes and raisins; stir until cereal is thoroughly coated. Press mixture into a buttered 8-inch square pan. Cool 30 mintues. Cut into squares.

Chocolate-Peanut Butter Krispies

Yield: about 3 dozen.

- 1 cup (6-ounce package) HERSHEY'S Semi-Sweet Chocolate Chips
- 1 cup REESE'S Peanut Butter Chips
- 2 tablespoons vegetable oil
- ½ cup chopped nuts
- 1⅓ cups crisp rice cereal

Combine chocolate chips, peanut butter chips and vegetable oil in the top of a double boiler over hot (not boiling) water. Stir until well blended and chips are completely melted. Remove from heat. Stir in nuts and cereal. Cool slightly. Drop by teaspoonfuls into decorative nut cups. Chill until firm. Store in covered container in refrigerator.

MIX COOKIES

Kids' Special Cookies

Yield: about 2½ dozen.

1 box (18.5 ounces) fudge marble cake mix
1 egg

⅓ cup vegetable oil
4 tablespoons water, divided
1 cup HERSHEY'S MINI CHIPS

Remove chocolate packet from cake mix box; set aside. Combine dry cake mix, egg, oil and 3 tablespoons of the water in large mixer bowl; beat until smooth. Stir in MINI CHIPS. Reserve ⅔ cup batter in a small mixing bowl. Add chocolate packet and remaining 1 tablespoon water to reserved batter; blend well. Drop vanilla batter by teaspoonfuls onto a greased cookie sheet. Spoon ½ teaspoonful of the chocolate batter on top of each vanilla cookie. Bake at 350° for 10 to 12 minutes or until golden. Remove from cookie sheet; cool on wire rack.

Quick Hide-and-Seek Cookies

Yield: about 32.

1 roll (17 ounces) refrigerated, unbaked sugar cookie dough
1 HERSHEY'S Milk Chocolate Bar (8 ounces)
⅔ cup finely chopped nuts

Cut cookie dough into ⅜-inch slices. Place on an ungreased cookie sheet. Let stand at room temperature 5 to 10 minutes to soften. Break chocolate bar into squares. Press a slice of cookie dough around each square, forming a ball that completely covers the chocolate. Roll balls in nuts to coat completely. Place on an ungreased cookie sheet. Bake at 375° for 10 to 12 minutes or until lightly browned. Cool slightly on cookie sheet. Remove from cookie sheet; cool completely on wire rack.

Quickie Fudge Squares

Yield: about 16.

2 ounces (2 blocks) HERSHEY'S Unsweetened Baking Chocolate
¼ cup butter *or* margarine
1 cup sugar

1 teaspoon vanilla
2 eggs, slightly beaten
1¼ cups buttermilk baking mix
½ cup chopped nuts

Melt chocolate and butter *or* margarine in a medium saucepan over low heat, stirring constantly. Blend in sugar, vanilla, eggs, buttermilk baking mix and nuts. (Batter may be lumpy.) Spread into a greased 8-inch square pan. Bake at 350° for 30 to 35 minutes or until set. Cool completely in pan. Cut into squares.

Kids' Special Cookies, above

MIX COOKIES

Quick and Easy Marbled Syrup Bars

Yield: about 16.

1 box (15 ounces) sugar cookie mix
½ cup (5.5-ounce can) HERSHEY'S
Syrup

Prepare cookie mix according to package directions. Spread batter into an ungreased 8-inch square pan. Pour chocolate syrup over top. Use a knife or metal spatula to turn syrup into cookie batter for a marbled effect. Bake at 375° for 25 to 30 minutes or until set. Cool completely in pan. Cut into bars.

Pudding Mix-Chocolate Chip Cookies

Yield: about 5½ dozen.

1 cup butter or margarine, softened
½ cup sugar
½ cup packed light brown sugar
1 package (3⅜ ounces) vanilla-flavored instant pudding and pie filling mix
2 eggs

2¼ cups unsifted all-purpose flour
1 teaspoon baking soda
2 cups (12-ounce package) HERSHEY'S Semi-Sweet Chocolate Chips
1 cup chopped walnuts, optional

Cream butter or margarine, both sugars and pudding and pie filling mix in large mixer bowl until light and fluffy. Add eggs; beat well. In a separate bowl, combine flour and baking soda; gradually add to creamed mixture; beat well. Stir in chocolate chips and nuts, if desired. Drop by teaspoonfuls onto an ungreased cookie sheet. Bake at 375° for 8 to 10 minutes or until lightly browned. Cool slightly on cookie sheet. Remove from cookie sheet; cool completely on wire rack.

Brownie Mix

Yield: about 10 cups.

4 cups unsifted all-purpose flour
3 cups sugar
2 cups nonfat dry milk powder

1 cup HERSHEY'S Cocoa
2 teaspoons baking powder
⅛ teaspoon salt

Combine all ingredients in a large mixing bowl; blend well. Store in a tightly covered container at room temperature until ready to use.

Brownies

Yield: about 16.

2½ cups Brownie Mix
¼ cup butter or margarine, melted
2 eggs

1 tablespoon water
1 teaspoon vanilla
½ cup chopped nuts

Combine all ingredients in a medium bowl; blend well. Pour batter into a greased 8-inch square pan. Bake at 350° for 20 to 25 minutes or until brownie begins to pull away from edges of pan. Cool completely in pan. Cut into squares.

Peanutty Chocolate Pastries

Yield: about 3½ dozen.

⅔ cup sugar
⅓ cup HERSHEY'S Cocoa
½ cup milk
2 cups (12-ounce package) REESE'S Peanut Butter Chips
1 teaspoon vanilla
½ cup chopped peanuts, optional

2 packages (11 ounces each) pie crust mix
¼ cup sugar
½ cup water
Milk
Confectioners' sugar, optional

Combine sugar and cocoa in a medium saucepan; blend in milk. Add peanut butter chips. Cook over low heat, stirring constantly, until chips are melted. Stir in vanilla and peanuts, if desired. Chill 20 minutes or until mixture is set. Meanwhile, in a medium bowl, combine pie crust mix, sugar and water. Mix until pastry holds together; shape into a smooth ball. Roll out about one quarter of the dough at a time ⅛ inch thick on a lightly floured pastry cloth. Cut into 2-inch circles. Place on an ungreased cookie sheet. Moisten edges with milk. Place 1 heaping teaspoon of the chilled filling in the center of each circle; cover with a second circle, stretching slightly to fit. Press edges together with fingers or fork tines. Brush tops with milk. Bake at 375° for 15 to 20 minutes. Remove from cookie sheet; cool on wire rack. Sprinkle with confectioners' sugar, if desired.

Chewy Syrup Bars

Yield: about 2½ dozen.

1 box (18.5 ounces) yellow cake mix
2 eggs
1 cup HERSHEY'S Syrup

1½ cups miniature marshmallows
¾ cup chopped nuts

Combine cake mix, eggs and syrup in large mixer bowl. Beat on high speed for 3 minutes or until well blended. Stir in marshmallows and nuts. Spread batter into a greased 13 × 9-inch pan. Bake at 350° for 40 to 45 minutes. Cool completely in pan. Cut into bars.

Easy Peanutty Snickerdoodles

Yield: about 2½ dozen.

1 package (15 ounces) sugar cookie mix
1 cup REESE'S Peanut Butter Chips

2 teaspoons cinnamon
2 tablespoons sugar

Prepare cookie mix according to package directions. Stir in peanut butter chips. In a small bowl, combine cinnamon and sugar; set aside. Shape dough into 1-inch balls. Roll balls in cinnamon-sugar mixture. Place on an ungreased cookie sheet. Bake at 375° for 8 to 10 minutes or until lightly browned. Cool slightly on cookie sheet. Remove from cookie sheet; cool completely on wire rack.

CANDY COOKIES

SPECIAL DARK Marble Slims

Yield: about 3 dozen.

6 tablespoons butter *or* margarine, softened
½ cup packed light brown sugar
¼ cup sugar
1 egg
½ teaspoon vanilla

1 cup unsifted all-purpose flour
½ teaspoon baking soda
½ teaspoon salt
3 HERSHEY'S SPECIAL DARK Bars (1.45 ounces each)
⅓ cup chopped nuts

Cream butter *or* margarine, both sugars, egg and vanilla in large mixer bowl until light and fluffy. In a separate bowl, combine flour, baking soda and salt; blend into creamed mixture. Spread batter into an ungreased 13 × 9-inch pan. Break chocolate bars into squares; scatter on top of batter. Bake at 350° for 3 minutes or *just* until chocolate is melted. Remove from oven. Use a spatula to gently swirl chocolate for a marbled effect. Sprinkle with nuts. Return to oven and bake 16 to 18 minutes or until lightly browned. Cool completely in pan. Cut into bars.

MR. GOODBAR Layer Cookies

Yield: about 2 dozen.

¼ cup butter *or* margarine
¾ cup vanilla wafer cookie crumbs
⅔ cup flaked coconut

1 HERSHEY'S MR. GOODBAR (8 ounces)
¾ cup sweetened condensed milk

Melt butter *or* margarine in an 8-inch square pan in a 350° oven. Sprinkle vanilla wafer crumbs evenly over butter *or* margarine in pan. Sprinkle coconut over cookie crumbs. Melt chocolate bar with condensed milk in the top of a double boiler over hot (not boiling) water, stirring occasionally until blended. Carefully spoon chocolate mixture over coconut; spread evenly. Bake at 350° for 30 minutes. Cool several hours or overnight. Cut into bars.

Chewy ROLO Cookie Bars

Yield: about 3 dozen.

1 package (18.5 ounces) yellow cake mix
½ cup chopped nuts

⅔ cup (5.3-ounce can) evaporated milk
¼ cup butter *or* margarine, melted
36 ROLO pieces, cut in half

Combine cake mix and nuts in a medium bowl. Stir in evaporated milk and melted butter *or* margarine; blend well. Spread about half of cake mixture into a greased 13 × 9-inch pan. Bake at 350° for 15 minutes. Remove from oven. Immediately place ROLO pieces, cut sides down, over hot crust. Drop remaining cake mixture by teaspoonfuls over ROLO pieces. Bake at 350° for 25 to 30 minutes or until lightly browned. Cool; cut into bars.

CANDY COOKIES

Chocolate Crumb Sandwich

Yield: about 16.

½ cup butter *or* margarine
½ cup packed light brown sugar
1½ cups graham cracker crumbs

1 HERSHEY'S Milk Chocolate Bar
  with Almonds (8 ounces)

Melt butter *or* margarine with brown sugar in small saucepan over medium heat, stirring occasionally until blended. Remove from heat. Add graham cracker crumbs; stir until crumbs are thoroughly moistened. Reserve 1 cup crumb mixture. Press remaining crumb mixture into a greased 8-inch square pan; set aside. Melt chocolate bar in the top of a double boiler over hot (not boiling) water. Spread evenly over crumb mixture in pan. Sprinkle reserved crumbs on top; press lightly into top. Let stand until cool. Cover and chill until firm. Cut into bars.

Candy Bar Crunch Cookies

Yield: about 6 dozen.

¾ cup peanut butter
½ cup shortening
1½ cups sugar
2 eggs
1 teaspoon vanilla
2 cups unsifted all-purpose flour

1 teaspoon baking powder
1 teaspoon salt
⅔ cup milk
4 HERSHEY'S MR. GOODBARS (2
  ounces each), cut into small pieces

Blend peanut butter and shortening in large mixer bowl. Gradually add sugar; cream until light and fluffy. Add eggs and vanilla; blend well. In a separate bowl, combine flour, baking powder and salt; add alternately with milk to creamed mixture; beat well. Stir in candy. Drop by tablespoonfuls onto a greased cookie sheet. Bake at 350° for 8 to 10 minutes or until lightly browned. Cool on wire rack.

REESE'S PIECES Chocolate Cookies

Yield: about 3½ dozen.

½ cup margarine *or* shortening,
  softened
1 cup sugar
1 egg
1 teaspoon vanilla
1½ cups unsifted all-purpose flour

⅓ cup HERSHEY'S Cocoa
½ teaspoon baking soda
½ teaspoon salt
¼ cup milk
1¼ cups REESE'S PIECES, divided

Cream margarine *or* shortening, sugar, egg and vanilla in large mixer bowl until light and fluffy. In a separate bowl, combine flour, cocoa, baking soda and salt; add alternately with milk to creamed mixture; beat well. Stir in ¾ cup of the REESE'S PIECES. Drop by teaspoonfuls onto an ungreased cookie sheet. Place 2 or 3 additional REESE'S PIECES near center of each cookie. Bake at 375° for 10 to 12 minutes or until almost set. *Do not overbake.* Cool 1 minute on cookie sheet. Remove from cookie sheet; cool completely on wire rack.

Peanut Butter Cup Cookies

Yield: about 40.

½ cup butter *or* margarine, softened
½ cup peanut butter
½ cup packed light brown sugar
¼ cup sugar
1 egg
1¾ cups unsifted all-purpose flour
1 teaspoon baking soda

⅛ teaspoon salt
1 egg white
1 tablespoon water
1 cup crushed corn flakes cereal
40 REESE'S Miniature Peanut Butter Cups (10-ounce package), paper liners removed.

Cream butter *or* margarine, peanut butter, and both sugars in large mixer bowl until light and fluffy. Add egg; beat well. In a separate bowl, combine flour, baking soda and salt; blend into creamed mixture. Shape dough into 1-inch balls. Combine egg white and water; beat with fork until foamy. Dip balls into egg white mixture, then into crushed cereal. Place on an ungreased cookie sheet. Press down with thumb in center to make a depression about 1 inch wide. Bake at 375° for 8 to 10 minutes or until set. Remove from oven. Immediately place a peanut butter cup in the center of each cookie. Cool on cookie sheet 1 minute. Carefully remove from cookie sheet; cool completely on wire rack.

Chocolate Bar Banana Squares

Yield: about 2 dozen.

⅓ cup shortening
¾ cup sugar
1 egg
1½ cups unsifted all-purpose flour
1½ teaspoons baking powder
¼ teaspoon baking soda
¼ teaspoon salt

1 cup mashed ripe bananas (about 3 medium)
¾ cup chopped nuts
2 HERSHEY'S MILK CHOCOLATE BARS (8 ounces each)
Vanilla Frosting (page 31), optional
Chopped nuts, optional

Cream shortening and sugar in small mixer bowl until light and fluffy. Add egg; beat well. In a separate bowl, combine flour, baking powder, baking soda and salt; add alternately with mashed bananas to creamed mixture; beat well. Stir in nuts. Spread 1⅓ cups of the batter into a greased 9-inch square pan. Bake at 350° for about 10 minutes or until set. Cool 10 minutes. Place chocolate bars, side by side and smooth side up, on cooled layer. (Small spaces around edges will fill in during baking.) Spread remaining batter evenly on top of chocolate bars, covering completely. Bake at 350° for 25 to 30 minutes or until center springs back when touched lightly. Cool completely in pan. Frost with Vanilla Frosting and sprinkle with chopped nuts, if desired.

MINI CHIP Sugar Cakes

Yield: about 3 dozen.

⅔ cup butter *or* margarine, softened
1½ cups packed light brown sugar
1 cup sugar
2 eggs
2 teaspoons vanilla
4½ cups unsifted all-purpose flour
2 teaspoons baking soda
1 teaspoon baking powder

1 teaspoon salt
1 cup buttermilk *or* sour milk*
2 cups (12-ounce package) HERSHEY'S MINI CHIPS
1 cup chopped walnuts, optional
Frosting, optional
Decorations, optional

Cream butter *or* margarine and both sugars in large mixer bowl until light and fluffy. Add eggs and vanilla; beat well. In a separate bowl, combine flour, baking soda, baking powder and salt; add alternately with buttermilk *or* sour milk to creamed mixture; beat well. Stir in MINI CHIPS and nuts, if desired. Drop by level quarter cupfuls onto a greased cookie sheet. Bake at 350° for 12 to 14 minutes or until lightly browned. Remove from cookie sheet; cool on wire rack. Frost and decorate, if desired.

To sour milk: Use 1 tablespoon vinegar plus milk to equal 1 cup.

Chocolate Finger Cookies

Yield: about 5 dozen.

1 cup butter *or* margarine, softened
1½ cups sugar
3 eggs
1 tablespoon vanilla
3¾ cups unsifted all-purpose flour

¾ cup HERSHEY'S Cocoa
¾ teaspoon baking soda
½ teaspoon salt
Chopped nuts and candied cherry halves, optional

Cream butter *or* margarine and sugar in large mixer bowl until light and fluffy. Add eggs and vanilla; beat well. In a separate bowl, combine flour, cocoa, baking soda and salt; gradually add to creamed mixture; beat well. Shape dough into 4 × ½-inch fingers. Place on an ungreased cookie sheet. Bake at 350° for 8 to 10 minutes or until almost set. Cool slightly on cookie sheet. Remove from cookie sheet; cool completely on wire rack. Glaze with Chocolate Glaze. Sprinkle with chopped nuts and garnish with candied cherry halves, if desired.

Chocolate Glaze

¼ cup butter *or* margarine
¼ cup water
6 tablespoons HERSHEY'S Cocoa

2 cups confectioners' sugar
1 teaspoon vanilla

Combine butter *or* margarine and water in a small saucepan; bring to a boil. Remove from heat. Immediately stir in cocoa. Add confectioners' sugar and vanilla; beat until smooth. (If too thick, add 1 to 2 teaspoons water.)

From top: MINI CHIP Sugar Cakes, above;
MINI CHIP Mandelschnitten, 64; Chocolate
Finger Cookies, above

HOLIDAY COOKIES

MINI CHIP Mandelschnitten

Yield: about 4 dozen.

1⅔ cups unsifted all-purpose flour
2 tablespoons sugar
¾ teaspoon baking powder
    Dash salt

½ cup chilled butter *or* margarine
1 egg, slightly beaten
2 tablespoons evaporated milk
1¼ cups HERSHEY'S MINI CHIPS

Combine flour, sugar, baking powder and salt in a medium bowl; cut in butter *or* margarine until mixture is the consistency of coarse crumbs. Stir in egg and evaporated milk; mix until pastry holds together. Gather into a ball. Roll out dough on a lightly floured pastry cloth into an 18 × 12-inch rectangle. Transfer to a 15½ × 10½ × 1-inch jelly-roll pan, easing into bottom and up sides of pan. Bake at 375° for 8 to 10 minutes or until browned. Cool completely in pan. Sprinkle with 1 cup MINI CHIPS; set aside. Prepare MINI CHIP Filling. Carefully spoon filling over baked crust. (Do not spread; mixture will spread during baking.) Bake at 375° for 12 to 15 minutes or until filling is caramel-colored. Sprinkle with ¼ cup MINI CHIPS. Cool in pan. Cut into bars.

Filling

1½ cups sugar
½ cup butter *or* margarine
½ cup evaporated milk

½ cup honey *or* light corn syrup
1½ cups sliced almonds

Combine sugar, butter *or* margarine, evaporated milk and honey *or* light corn syrup in a 3-quart saucepan. Cook over medium heat, stirring constantly, until mixture comes to a boil. Stir in almonds. Cook and stir over medium heat until mixture reaches 240° F. (soft-ball stage). Remove from heat.

Blue Ribbon Fruit Cookies

Yield: about 4 dozen.

¾ cup butter *or* margarine, melted
1½ cups packed light brown sugar
4 eggs
4 blocks (4 ounces) HERSHEY'S
    Unsweetened Baking Chocolate
2 cups unsifted all-purpose flour

2 teaspoons baking powder
1 teaspoon salt
½ teaspoon cinnamon
1 cup candied pineapple chunks
1 cup raisins
1 cup chopped nuts

Combine melted butter *or* margarine and brown sugar in large mixer bowl; blend well. Add eggs; beat well. Melt baking chocolate in the top of a double boiler over hot (not boiling) water; add to egg-sugar mixture. In a separate bowl, combine flour, baking powder, salt and cinnamon; gradually add to chocolate mixture. Stir in candied pineapple, raisins and nuts. Drop by teaspoonfuls onto a lightly greased cookie sheet. Bake at 350° for 8 to 10 mintues or until almost set. Cool slightly on cookie sheet. Remove from cookie sheet; cool completely on wire rack.

Peanut Butter Heart Cookies

Yield: about 5 dozen.

2 cups (12-ounce package) REESE'S Peanut Butter Chips
½ cup margarine (Do *not* use butter.)
1 cup sugar
2 eggs
2 teaspoons vanilla

2 cups unsifted all-purpose flour
1½ teaspoons baking soda
½ teaspoon salt
Colored decorator frostings and gels

Melt peanut butter chips in the top of a double boiler over hot (not boiling) water, stirring until smooth. Cream margarine and sugar in large mixer bowl until light and fluffy. Add eggs and vanilla; beat well. Blend in melted peanut butter chips. In a separate bowl, combine flour, baking soda and salt; blend into creamed mixture. Cover tightly; chill 1 hour or until firm enough to handle. Divide dough into quarters. Roll out each quarter ¼ inch thick between 2 pieces of waxed paper. Cut into heart shapes with a cookie cutter. Place on an ungreased cookie sheet. Bake at 375° for 6 to 8 minutes or until almost set. Cool slightly on cookie sheet. Remove from cookie sheet; cool completely on wire rack. Frost and decorate as desired.

Valentine Sandwiches

Divide chilled dough into quarters. Roll out each quarter ¼ inch thick between 2 pieces of waxed paper. Cut out half of dough with a 2-inch round cookie cutter. Cut out remaining half with a 2-inch doughnut cutter. Place on an ungreased cookie sheet. Bake at 375° for 6 to 8 minutes or until almost set. Cool slightly on cookie sheet. Remove from cookie sheet; cool completely on wire rack. Prepare Strawberry Cream Filling. Spread filling on one solid round; top with open round. Fill centers with additional strawberry preserves, if desired. Yield: about 3 dozen.

Strawberry Creme Filling

¼ cup butter *or* margarine, softened
2 cups confectioners' sugar
2 tablespoons milk

2 tablespoons strawberry preserves
Red food color

Combine butter *or* margarine, confectioners' sugar, milk and strawberry preserves in small mixer bowl; beat until creamy. Stir in food color for darker color, if desired.

French Chocolate Meringues

Yield: about 3 dozen.

3 egg whites
⅛ teaspoon cream of tartar
¾ cup sugar

1 teaspoon almond extract
1 cup HERSHEY'S MINI CHIPS
1 cup slivered almonds

Beat egg whites and cream of tartar in small mixer bowl until foamy. Gradually add sugar, beating until stiff peaks form. Blend in almond extract. Fold in MINI CHIPS and nuts. Drop by teaspoonfuls onto a lightly greased cookie sheet. Bake at 350° for 15 to 20 minutes or until lightly browned. Cool 1 minute on cookie sheet. Remove from cookie sheet; cool completely on wire rack.

HOLIDAY COOKIES

Petite Chocolate Tarts

Yield: about 4 dozen.

2 packages (3 ounces each) cream
   cheese, softened
½ cup butter *or* margarine, softened

½ cup shortening
2 cups unsifted all-purpose flour

Blend cream cheese, butter *or* margarine and shortening in large mixer bowl. Gradually add flour; beat well. Cover tightly; chill about 1 hour or until firm enough to handle. Shape dough into 48 1-inch balls. Place in ungreased 1¾-inch muffin cups. Press balls against the bottom and up the side of each muffin cup; set aside. Prepare Spiked Filling. Spoon a heaping teaspoonful of Filling into each pastry shell. Bake at 350° for 20 to 25 minutes. Cool; remove from pan. Garnish with a dollop of Topping, if desired.

Spiked Filling

2 eggs
1 cup sugar
3 tablespoons cornstarch
½ cup butter *or* margarine, melted

¼ cup bourbon *or* apple juice
¾ cup HERSHEY'S MINI CHIPS
½ cup finely chopped pecans

Beat eggs slightly in small mixer bowl; gradually add sugar and cornstarch. Add melted butter *or* margarine and bourbon *or* apple juice; blend well. Stir in MINI CHIPS and nuts.

Topping

⅔ cup heavy cream
¼ cup confectioners' sugar
1 to 2 teaspoons bourbon

Beat all ingredients in small mixer bowl until stiff peaks form. For a quick variation, substitute 1⅓ cups whipped topping for heavy cream and confectioners' sugar; blend in bourbon.

Yule Jewels

Yield: about 3 dozen.

⅓ cup butter *or* margarine, softened
2 tablespoons sugar
1 egg
1 package (8 ounces) white *or* yellow
   cake mix
1 cup (6-ounce package) HERSHEY'S
   Semi-Sweet Chocolate Chips

½ cup red candied cherries, cut into
   quarters
½ cup green candied cherries, cut into
   quarters
½ cup candied pineapple chunks

Cream butter *or* margarine and sugar in large mixer bowl until light and fluffy. Add egg; beat well. Gradually add cake mix, blending until smooth. Stir in chocolate chips, both colors cherries and pineapple. Drop by teaspoonfuls onto an ungreased cookie sheet. Bake at 375° for 10 to 12 minutes or until lightly browned. Cool slightly on cookie sheet. Remove from cookie sheet; cool completely on wire rack.

Valentine Sandwiches, 65;
Petite Chocolate Tarts, above

HOLIDAY COOKIES

Sugar-Frosted Cocoa Cookies

Yield: about 6 dozen.

- 1 cup butter *or* margarine, softened
- 2 cups sugar
- 2 eggs
- ½ cup milk
- 2 teaspoons vanilla
- 3 cups unsifted all-purpose flour
- 1 cup HERSHEY'S Cocoa
- 1 teaspoon baking soda
- 1 teaspoon salt
- Sugar
- Walnut halves

Cream butter *or* margarine, sugar and eggs in large mixer bowl until light and fluffy. Add milk and vanilla; beat well. In a separate bowl, combine flour, cocoa, baking soda and salt; gradually add to creamed mixture; beat well. Shape into 1-inch balls. (If dough is too soft, cover and chill about 30 minutes.) Roll balls in sugar to coat completely. Garnish with walnut halves. Place on an ungreased cookie sheet. Bake at 375° for 8 to 10 minutes or until almost no imprint remains when touched lightly. Remove from cookie sheet; cool on wire rack.

Peanut Butter Chip Mincemeat Drops

Yield: about 4½ dozen.

- ½ cup butter *or* margarine, softened
- 1 cup sugar
- 3 eggs
- 2¾ cups unsifted all-purpose flour
- 2 teaspoons baking soda
- 1 teaspoon salt
- 1 cup prepared mincemeat
- 1 cup REESE'S Peanut Butter Chips

Cream butter *or* margarine and sugar in large mixer bowl until light and fluffy. Add eggs; beat well. In a separate bowl, combine flour, baking soda and salt; gradually add to creamed mixture. Stir in mincemeat and peanut butter chips. Drop by teaspoonfuls onto a lightly greased cookie sheet. Bake at 350° for 10 to 12 minutes or until lightly browned. Remove from cookie sheet; cool on wire rack.

Cocoa Press Cookies

Yield: about 4½ dozen.

- 1 cup butter *or* margarine, softened
- ⅔ cup sugar
- 1 egg
- 1 teaspoon vanilla
- 2¼ cups unsifted all-purpose flour
- ⅓ cup HERSHEY'S Cocoa
- ½ teaspoon salt

Cream butter *or* margarine, sugar, egg and vanilla in large mixer bowl until light and fluffy. In a separate bowl, combine flour, cocoa and salt; gradually add to creamed mixture. Fill a cookie press with dough. Press cookies onto cool, ungreased cookie sheet. Bake at 350° for 5 to 7 minutes or until set. Remove from cookie sheet; cool on wire rack.

Peanut Butter Chip Pumpkin Cookies

Yield: about 6 dozen.

- 1 cup butter *or* margarine, softened
- 2 cups packed light brown sugar
- 2 eggs
- 2 cups canned pumpkin
- 2 teaspoons vanilla
- 4 cups unsifted all-purpose flour
- 2 teaspoons baking powder
- 2 teaspoons cinnamon
- 1 teaspoon baking soda
- 1 teaspoon nutmeg
- 2 cups (12-ounce package) REESE'S Peanut Butter Chips
- 1 cup raisins

Cream butter *or* margarine and brown sugar in large mixer bowl until light and fluffy. Add eggs, pumpkin and vanilla; beat well. In a separate bowl, combine flour, baking powder, cinnamon, baking soda and nutmeg; gradually add to pumpkin mixture; beat well. Stir in peanut butter chips and raisins. Drop by teaspoonfuls onto a greased cookie sheet. Bake at 375° for 10 to 12 minutes or until lightly browned. Remove from cookie sheet; cool on wire rack. Frost with Peanut Butter Chip Frosting.

Peanut Butter Chip Frosting

- ½ cup butter *or* margarine
- 6 tablespoons milk
- 1½ cups REESE'S Peanut Butter Chips
- 2 cups confectioners' sugar
- 1 teaspoon vanilla

Combine butter *or* margarine, milk and peanut butter chips in a small saucepan. Cook over low heat, stirring constantly, until chips are melted and mixture is smooth. Immediately add heated mixture to confectioners' sugar and vanilla in a small mixer bowl; beat until smooth. Spread while frosting is warm.

Cocoa-Coconut Gems

Yield: about 2 dozen.

- 1 package (3 ounces) cream cheese, softened
- ½ cup butter *or* margarine, softened
- 1 cup unsifted all-purpose flour

Blend cream cheese and butter *or* margarine in small bowl. Blend in flour. Cover and chill 1 hour. Shape dough into 24 1-inch balls. Place in ungreased 1¾-inch muffin cups. Press balls evenly against the bottom and up the sides of each muffin cup; set aside. Prepare Coconut Filling. Spoon 2 level teaspoonfuls of Coconut Filling into each pastry shell. Bake at 350° for 20 to 25 minutes or until set. Cool. Remove from pans. Garnish each with a dollop of whipped cream, if desired.

Coconut Filling

- 1 egg, slightly beaten
- ½ cup sugar
- 3 tablespoons butter *or* margarine, melted
- ¼ cup HERSHEY'S Cocoa
- ½ teaspoon vanilla
- ½ cup flaked coconut

Combine egg, sugar, butter *or* margarine, cocoa and vanilla in small bowl; stir just until smooth. Stir in coconut.

HERSHEY'S CLASSICS

Crunchy MR. GOODBAR Squares

Yield: about 2 dozen.

⅓ cup butter *or* margarine, softened
⅓ cup confectioners' sugar
1 egg yolk
⅔ cup unsifted all-purpose flour
2 eggs
1 teaspoon vanilla
1 cup sugar
2 tablespoons unsifted all-purpose flour

1 teaspoon baking powder
½ teaspoon salt
1 cup quick-cooking oats
¾ cup flaked coconut
2 HERSHEY'S MR. GOODBARS (8 ounces each)
25 maraschino cherry halves, well drained

Cream butter *or* margarine, confectioners' sugar and egg yolk in small mixer bowl until light and fluffy. Add ⅔ cup flour; blend well. Spread batter evenly into a greased 9-inch square pan. (Layer will be thin.) Bake at 350° for 10 minutes; cool 10 minutes. Meanwhile, beat eggs slightly in small mixer bowl; blend in vanilla. In a separate bowl, combine sugar, 2 tablespoons flour, baking powder and salt; gradually add to beaten eggs. Stir in oats and coconut. Place chocolate bars, peanut side up, on cooled layer. (Small spaces around edges will fill in during baking.) Spread coconut mixture on top of chocolate layer, covering chocolate completely. Arrange cherry halves on top. Bake at 350° for 30 to 35 minutes or until lightly browned. Cool; cut into bars.

Macaroon KISS Cookies

Yield: about 4½ dozen.

⅓ cup butter *or* margarine, softened
1 package (3 ounces) cream cheese, softened
¾ cup sugar
1 egg yolk
2 teaspoons almond extract
2 teaspoons orange juice

1¼ cups unsifted all-purpose flour
2 teaspoons baking powder
¼ teaspoon salt
5 cups (14-ounce package) flaked coconut, divided
54 HERSHEY'S KISSES

Cream butter *or* margarine, cream cheese and sugar in large mixer bowl until light and fluffy. Add egg yolk, almond extract and orange juice; beat well. In a separate bowl, combine flour, baking powder and salt; gradually add to creamed mixture. Stir in 3 cups of the flaked coconut. Cover bowl tightly; chill at least 1 hour. Shape dough into 1-inch balls. Roll balls in remaining 2 cups coconut to coat completely. Place on an ungreased cookie sheet. Bake at 350° for 10 to 12 minutes or until lightly browned. Press an unwrapped KISS in center of each cookie. Cool 1 minute on cookie sheet. Carefully remove from cookie sheet; cool completely on wire rack.

HERSHEY'S CLASSICS

S'Mores

Yield: about 2 dozen.

¾ cup butter *or* margarine, softened
⅔ cup sugar
1 egg
1 teaspoon vanilla
3 cups graham cracker crumbs
½ cup unsifted all-purpose flour

½ teaspoon salt
9 HERSHEY'S Milk Chocolate Bars (1.45 ounces each)
1 egg white
3½ cups miniature marshmallows

Cream butter *or* margarine and sugar in large mixer bowl until light and fluffy. Add egg and vanilla; beat well. Stir in graham cracker crumbs, flour and salt. Reserve 2 cups of graham cracker mixture. Press remaining mixture into a greased 13 × 9-inch pan. Place single layer of chocolate bars on top. Beat egg white until foamy; stir in marshmallows. Spread on top of chocolate bars. Press reserved mixture on top of marshmallows. Bake at 350° for 30 minutes. Cool 10 minutes; cut into bars.

Peanut Butter and Jelly Bars

Yield: about 16.

1½ cups unsifted all-purpose flour
½ cup sugar
¾ teaspoon baking powder
½ cup chilled butter *or* margarine

1 egg, slightly beaten
¾ cup grape jelly
1 cup REESE'S Peanut Butter Chips, divided

Combine flour, sugar and baking powder in a large mixing bowl. Cut in butter *or* margarine until mixture is the consistency of coarse crumbs. Add egg; blend well. Reserve half of mixture. Press remaining half of mixture into a greased 9-inch square pan. Spread grape jelly evenly over crust in pan. Sprinkle ½ cup of the peanut butter chips over jelly. Combine reserved crumb mixture with remaining ½ cup chips; sprinkle over top. Bake at 375° for 30 minutes or until lightly browned. Cool; cut into bars.

Hide-and-Seek Peanut Butter Cups

Yield: about 2½ dozen.

½ cup shortening (Do *not* substitute butter or margarine.)
½ cup packed light brown sugar
¼ cup sugar
½ teaspoon vanilla
1 egg

1½ cups unsifted all-purpose flour
½ teaspoon baking soda
30 REESE'S Miniature Peanut Butter Cups
1 cup chopped peanuts

Cream shortening, both sugars and vanilla in large mixer bowl until light and fluffy. Add egg; beat well. In a separate bowl, combine flour and baking soda; gradually add to creamed mixture. Press about 1 tablespoon around each peanut butter cup. Roll in chopped nuts. Place on an ungreased cookie sheet. Bake at 375° for 10 to 12 minutes or until lightly browned. Cool on wire rack.

Peanut Butter Chip Filled Chocolate Cookies

Yield: about 16.

½ cup shortening
1 cup sugar
1 egg
1 teaspoon vanilla
1¾ cups unsifted all-purpose flour

½ cup HERSHEY'S Cocoa
1¼ teaspoons baking soda
⅛ teaspoon salt
1 cup buttermilk *or* sour milk*

Cream shortening and sugar in large mixer bowl until light and fluffy. Add egg and vanilla; beat well. In a separate bowl, combine flour, cocoa, baking soda and salt; add alternately with buttermilk or sour milk to creamed mixture; beat well. Drop by tablespoonfuls onto a lightly greased cookie sheet. Bake at 375° for 10 to 12 minutes or until cookie springs back when touched lightly in center. Remove from cookie sheet; cool on wire rack. Spread flat side of 1 cookie with Peanut Butter Filling; top with a second cookie.

To sour milk: Use 1 tablespoon vinegar plus milk to equal 1 cup.

Peanut Butter Filling

1 cup REESE'S Peanut Butter Chips
1 tablespoon shortening (do *not* substitute butter or margarine)
1 package (8 ounces) cream cheese, softened

⅛ teaspoon salt
½ teaspoon vanilla
2½ cups confectioners' sugar

Melt peanut butter chips and shortening in the top of a double boiler over hot (not boiling) water. Combine melted peanut butter chip mixture, cream cheese, salt and vanilla in small mixer bowl; beat until smooth. Gradually add confectioners' sugar; beat until smooth. (If too thick, stir in ½ teaspoon milk at a time, until filling is of spreading consistency.)

Secret KISS Cookies

Yield: about 3 dozen.

1 cup butter *or* margarine, softened
½ cup sugar
1 teaspoon vanilla
1¾ cups unsifted all-purpose flour

1 cup finely chopped walnuts
36 HERSHEY'S KISSES
Confectioners' sugar

Cream butter *or* margarine, sugar and vanilla in large mixer bowl until light and fluffy. Gradually add flour and nuts; beat on low speed until well blended. Cover bowl tightly; chill at least 1 hour. Shape about 1 tablespoon dough around each unwrapped KISS. Be sure to cover KISS completely. Place on an ungreased cookie sheet. Bake 10 to 12 minutes or until set. Cool slightly on cookie sheet. Remove from cookie sheet; cool completely on wire rack. Roll in confectioners' sugar while still warm. Cool completely. Roll again in confectioners' sugar before serving, if desired.

Peanut Butter Chip Chocolate Cookies

Yield: about 5 dozen.

1 cup butter *or* margarine, softened
1½ cups sugar
2 eggs
2 teaspoons vanilla
2 cups unsifted all-purpose flour

⅔ cup HERSHEY'S Cocoa
¾ teaspoon baking soda
½ teaspoon salt
2 cups (12-ounce package) REESE'S Peanut Butter Chips

Cream butter *or* margarine, sugar, eggs and vanilla in large mixer bowl until light and fluffy. In a separate bowl, combine flour, cocoa, baking soda and salt; gradually add to creamed mixture. Stir in peanut butter chips. Drop by teaspoonfuls onto an ungreased cookie sheet. Bake at 350° for 8 to 10 minutes. Cool 1 minute on cookie sheet. Remove from cookie sheet; cool completely on wire rack.

Peanut Butter Chip Cookies

Yield: about 5 dozen.

1 cup shortening*
1 cup sugar
½ cup packed light brown sugar
1 teaspoon vanilla
2 eggs

2 cups unsifted all-purpose flour
1 teaspoon baking soda
2 cups (12-ounce package) REESE'S Peanut Butter Chips

Cream shortening, both sugars and vanilla in large mixer bowl until light and fluffy. Add eggs; beat well. In a separate bowl, combine flour and baking soda; gradually add to creamed mixture. Stir in peanut butter chips. Drop by teaspoonfuls onto an ungreased cookie sheet. Bake at 350° for 10 to 12 minutes or until lightly browned. Cool slightly on cookie sheet. Remove from cookie sheet; cool completely on wire rack.

*If desired, ¾ cup butter *or* margarine, softened, can be substituted.

Crunchy REESE'S PIECES Cookies

Yield: about 6 dozen.

1 cup shortening
1 cup packed light brown sugar
½ cup sugar
1 teaspoon vanilla
2 eggs

2½ cups unsifted all-purpose flour
1 teaspoon baking soda
1 teaspoon salt
2 cups (1-pound package) REESE'S PIECES

Cream shortening, both sugars and vanilla in large mixer bowl until light and fluffy. Add eggs; beat well. In a separate bowl, combine flour, baking soda and salt; gradually add to creamed mixture. Stir in REESE'S PIECES. Cover tightly; chill at least 1 hour. Drop by teaspoonfuls onto an ungreased cookie sheet. Bake at 375° for 8 to 10 minutes or until lightly browned. Cool slightly on cookie sheet. Remove from cookie sheet; cool completely on wire rack.

HERSHEY'S CLASSICS

Peanut Butter and Chocolate Chip Pan Cookies

Yield: about 3 dozen.

- 1 cup butter *or* margarine, softened
- ¾ cup packed light brown sugar
- ¾ cup sugar
- 1 teaspoon vanilla
- 2 eggs
- 2¼ cups unsifted all-purpose flour
- 1 teaspoon baking soda
- ½ teaspoon salt
- 1 cup HERSHEY'S Semi-Sweet Chocolate Chips, Milk Chocolate Chips *or* MINI CHIPS
- 1 cup REESE'S Peanut Butter Chips

Cream butter *or* margarine, both sugars and vanilla in large mixer bowl until light and fluffy. Add eggs; beat well. In a separate bowl, combine flour, baking soda and salt; gradually add to creamed mixture. Stir in chocolate chips and peanut butter chips. Spread evenly into a greased 15½ × 10½ × 1-inch jelly-roll pan. Bake at 375° for 20 minutes. Cool completely in pan. Cut into bars.

REESE'S® Cookies

Yield: about 5 dozen.

- 1 cup shortening*
- 1 cup sugar
- ½ cup packed light brown sugar
- 1 teaspoon vanilla
- 2 eggs
- 2 cups unsifted all-purpose flour
- 1 teaspoon baking soda
- 1 cup REESE'S Peanut Butter Chips
- 1 cup HERSHEY'S Semi-Sweet Chocolate Chips

Cream shortening, both sugars and vanilla in large mixer bowl until light and fluffy. Add eggs; beat well. Combine flour and baking soda; add to creamed mixture. Stir in peanut butter chips and chocolate chips. Drop by teaspoonfuls onto an ungreased cookie sheet. Bake at 350° for 10 to 12 minutes or until lightly browned. Cool slightly; remove from cookie sheet onto wire rack. Cool completely.

*If desired, ¾ cup butter *or* margarine, softened, can be substituted.

1982 Hershey Foods Corporation

Cocoa KISS Cookies

Yield: about 4½ dozen.

- 1 cup butter *or* margarine, softened
- ⅔ cup sugar
- 1 teaspoon vanilla
- 1⅔ cups unsifted all-purpose flour
- ¼ cup HERSHEY'S Cocoa
- 1 cup finely chopped pecans
- 54 HERSHEY'S KISSES
- Confectioners' sugar

Cream butter *or* margarine, sugar and vanilla in large mixer bowl until light and fluffy. In a separate bowl, combine flour and cocoa; blend into creamed mixture. Add nuts; beat on low speed until well blended. Chill dough 1 hour or until firm enough to handle. Press a scant tablespoon of dough around each unwrapped KISS. Shape into balls. Place on an ungreased cookie sheet. Bake at 375° for 10 to 12 minutes or until almost set. Cool slightly on cookie sheet. Remove from cookie sheet; cool completely on wire rack. Roll in confectioners' sugar to coat completely.

HERSHEY BAR Squares

Yield: about 2 dozen.

½ cup butter *or* margarine, softened
½ cup sugar
¼ cup packed light brown sugar
1 cup unsifted all-purpose flour
¾ cup quick-cooking oats
¼ teaspoon baking soda
¼ teaspoon salt
1 HERSHEY'S Milk Chocolate Bar (8 ounces)
1 tablespoon shortening

Cream butter *or* margarine and both sugars in small mixer bowl until light and fluffy. In a separate bowl, combine flour, oats, baking soda and salt; gradually add to creamed mixture. (Mixture will be crumbly.) Reserve ¾ cup crumb mixture for topping. Pat remaining crumbs evenly into a greased 8-inch square pan. Bake at 350° for 15 minutes. Meanwhile, melt milk chocolate bar and shortening in the top of a double boiler over hot (not boiling) water; blend well. Spread evenly on top of the hot baked cookie layer. Sprinkle reserved crumbs evenly over top of melted chocolate. Gently press crumbs into chocolate with back of spoon. Return to oven and bake 10 minutes or until lightly browned. Cool completely in pan. Cut into squares.

Peanut Butter and Jelly Thumbprints

Yield: about 5 dozen.

1 cup butter *or* margarine, softened
1¾ cups packed light brown sugar
2 eggs
2 teaspoons vanilla
3 cups unsifted all-purpose flour
1 teaspoon baking powder
1 teaspoon salt
1½ cups quick-cooking oats
2 cups (12-ounce package) REESE'S Peanut Butter Chips
¾ cup any jelly *or* preserves

Cream butter *or* margarine and brown sugar in large mixer bowl until light and fluffy. Add eggs and vanilla; beat well. In a separate bowl, combine flour, baking powder and salt; gradually add to creamed mixture. Reserve ½ cup of the peanut butter chips. Stir in oats and remaining 1½ cups peanut butter chips. Shape dough into 1-inch balls. Place on an ungreased cookie sheet. Press down with thumb in center to make a deep depression. Bake at 400° for 7 to 9 minutes or until lightly browned. Remove from cookie sheet; cool on wire rack. Fill center of each cookie with ½ teaspoon jelly *or* preserves. Top with several of the reserved peanut butter chips.

HERSHEY'S Traditional Chocolate Chip Cookies

Yield: about 6 dozen.

- 1 cup butter *or* margarine, softened
- ¾ cup sugar
- ¾ cup packed light brown sugar
- 1 teaspoon vanilla
- 2 eggs
- 2¼ cups unsifted all-purpose flour
- 1 teaspoon baking soda
- ½ teaspoon salt
- 2 cups (12-ounce package) HERSHEY'S Semi-Sweet Chocolate Chips
- 1 cup chopped nuts, optional

Cream butter *or* margarine, both sugars and vanilla in large mixer bowl until light and fluffy. Add eggs; beat well. In a separate bowl, combine flour, baking soda and salt; gradually add to creamed mixture. Stir in chocolate chips and nuts, if desired. Drop by teaspoonfuls onto an ungreased cookie sheet. Bake at 375° for 8 to 10 minutes or until lightly browned. Cool slightly on cookie sheet. Remove from cookie sheet; cool completely on wire rack.

Peanut Blossoms

Yield: about 4 dozen.

- ½ cup shortening
- ¾ cup peanut butter
- ⅓ cup sugar
- ⅓ cup packed light brown sugar
- 1 egg
- 2 tablespoons milk
- 1 teaspoon vanilla
- 1½ cups unsifted all-purpose flour
- 1 teaspoon baking soda
- ½ teaspoon salt
- Sugar
- 54 HERSHEY'S KISSES

Blend shortening and peanut butter in large mixer bowl. Add both sugars; cream until light and fluffy. Add egg, milk and vanilla; beat well. In a separate bowl, combine flour, baking soda and salt; gradually add to creamed mixture. Shape dough into 1-inch balls. Roll balls in sugar. Place on an ungreased cookie sheet. Bake at 375° for 10 to 12 minutes or until lightly browned. Immediately place an unwrapped KISS on top of each cookie, pressing down so that cookie cracks around the edges. Remove from cookie sheet; cool on wire rack.

1. Cocoa Coconut Gems, 69 2. Best Brownies, 36 3. Macaroon KISS Cookies, 70
4. Peanut Butter and Jelly Thumbprints, 77
5. Peanut Butter Chip Chocolate Filled Cookies, 73

Index

A
B
C
D
E
F
G
H
I
J
K
L

3
4
5
6
7
8
9
0
1